NOMADS

Nomadic Material Culture

In the Asian Collections

of the Horniman Museum

Contributions in Critical Museology and Material Culture.

NOMADS

Nomadic Material Culture
In the Asian Collections
of the Horniman Museum

Ken Teague

 The Horniman Museum and Gardens, London

 Museu Antroplógico da Universidade de Coimbra

Contributions in Critical Museology and Material Culture is produced by the Horniman Museum and Gardens, London and the Museu Antropológico da Universidade de Coimbra.

Series Editors
Anthony Shelton, Horniman Museum, London
Paulo Gama Mota, Universidade de Coimbra

Editorial Board
Karel Arnaut, University of Gent
Mary Bouquet, University of Utrecht
Nélia Dias, Instituto Superior Das Ciêcias do
      Trabalho e da Empresa, Lisbon
Pieter ter Keurs, Rijksmuseum voor
      Volkenkunde, Leiden
Frances Palmer, Royal College of Music,
      London
Nuno Porto, Universidade de Coimbra
Mike Rowlands, University College, London

Production
Daria Neklesa

With special thanks to the staff at Macmillan General Books and Stuart Laidlaw from the Institute of Archaeology, University College London.

Set in Adobe Garamond 10.5/14.5
Printed in Singapore
© The Horniman Museum and Gardens, London,
The Museu Antropológico da Universidade de Coimbra
Ken Teague, 2000

ISBN 0-9518141-6-8

Contents

Illustrations

Maps

Foreword

Nomadic material culture from Asian societies is not generally well represented in museum collections in Britain. This is particularly so regarding collections from those countries of Inner Asia which were formerly under the influence of the U.S.S.R., and so were less accessible to western European curators and collectors. It is therefore pleasing to welcome this publication of the Horniman Museum's collections from peoples of Inner and Western Asia where nomadism has been, and in some cases remains, a characteristic element of economy and society.

Staff at the Horniman Museum have had a long-standing interest in nomadic material culture, not only from Inner Asia but on a world-wide basis throughout most of the twentieth century. Ken Teague, curator of the Asian Ethnographic collections at the Horniman Museum for the last twenty-five years, has carried out an impressive programme of systematic collecting and research in this field. This active collecting policy has led to a unique collection of tents and their furnishings, amongst other significant material, which it is becoming ever more difficult to collect and document from an increasingly marginalised section of contemporary life. This programme continues to be effected in collaboration with colleagues in the Horniman and other museums on a current project in Central Asia.

Jane Wilkinson
Curator East Asian Collections
National Museums of Scotland

Figure 1: A family dismantling their yurt in Kyrgyzstan 1998. (Photograph: Ken Teague)

Preface

The collections discussed here have been compiled by curators and their agents (usually friends) over the course of the last century, in my own case for the last twenty-five years as Curator of the Asian Ethnographic Collections at the Horniman Museum. The Museum has an active collecting policy so that these collections are part of an on-going process of development. This Occasional Paper is intended to survey and publicise the Museum's collections of the material culture of particular societies which have nomadism as a significant aspect in their economy, social organisation and culture. These societies, which are discussed as a series of case histories consist of the Mongols, Kyrgyz, Iranian (Shah Sevan), Turkish and Tibetan nomads, who exemplify peoples living in the two main tent types of this region: the trellis tent and the black-hair velum tent. The nomadic peoples of the world are an endangered minority. Their representation by objects and information is thus vitally important for the understanding of the different lifestyles of humanity.

Acknowledgments

Acknowledgments are due to former and present Trustees of the Horniman Museum, to successive Directors: David Boston, Mike Houlihan and Janet Vitmayer, and to colleagues on the Museum's staff, especially Anthony Shelton, for supporting this endeavour; also to numerous others including Peter Andrews for the Shah Sevan Collection, to Richard Tapper for the Shah Sevan photographs; to Anthony Aris for the Eastern Tibetan Collection; to Stephanie Bunn for acting as a guide and for help in making the Kyrgyz Collection; to Tsering Chodak for Tibetan material and information; to Caroline Humphrey for permission to use her article on the Mongolian *ger*; to Daria Neklesa for chasing the production; to Nicky and Katie Levell for help with the maps; to Hakan Tazecan for the Turkish Collection; to N. Tsultem for the Mongolian Collection; to Michael Vickers for the map on Scythia; to Jane Wilkinson for collaborative professional support and long-standing friendship; and to my wife Louise for almost every sort of encouragement and help.

Ken Teague

Nomads, Material Culture and Museums

1

Nomadic peoples now form less than one percent of the world's population, with many still under considerable pressure to abandon their lifestyles. For this reason the study and acquisition of nomadic material culture has been given a high priority in the research carried out at the Horniman Museum over more than ninety years.

The brief of the Horniman Museum is to examine the relationship between peoples and their environments. The Horniman's ethnographic collections are structured according to the Blackwood system (1970), which classifies objects according to themes based on the major activities in human life, largely in pre-industrial societies; a scheme which facilitates a comparative perspective on material culture. The boundaries of such activities are deliberately held open rather than being sharply defined to allow flexibility in approach, and the future inclusion of additional objects and information. This systematic structure permits both wide-range sampling of activities such as 'nomadism', which may be represented, compared and analysed in greater or lesser depth in particular social or cultural cases.[1]

This paper deals with the Horniman Museum's collections of material culture drawn from several nomadic societies in Inner and Western Asia. These collections, number about 1,500 to 2,000 objects, and largely date from the last century, but they also contain small amounts of archaeological material dating from the first millennium BC, from Scythia, Luristan and China, which provide a counterweight to the tendency to deal with ethnographic collections in terms of types of societies in a questionable 'ethnographic present.'

The collections have been compiled by successive curators and their agents at the Horniman Museum, which indicates our continuing interest in nomadic societies over the last century. The Museum has an active policy of field collecting. In the execution of this approach as Curator of the Asian collections, I have been engaged in collecting nomadic material since 1979, and undertook field trips in Mongolia (1979, 1990, 1992), Turkey (1989, 1990, 1993, 1994), Uzbekistan (1997, 1998) and Kyrgyzstan (1998). Future fieldwork is planned to extend this work in further areas in Central Asia.

The collections of nomadic material fall into substantial and partial collections representing peoples who dwell in the two main tent types: felt covered trellis tents, and black hair velum tents. Felt tent peoples include the Mongols, Shah Sevan and Turks, with lesser collections from the Kyrgyz, Kazak and Iranian Turkomen. Black tent nomads are represented substantially in the Turkish and Tibetan collections, with lesser, linking collections from Kurdish, Arabian and Baluch peoples. Although the tents and their furnishings all date from the 20th century, they represent types which have been in use for centuries and are still currently used; reminding us that nomadism is by no means a lifestyle of the past.

After outlining the early history of nomadism and its representation through the collections (Chapters 2 - 3), I discuss the collections from the societies listed above in their particular historical and social contexts (Chapters 4 - 8), to provide a basis for limited comparisons. The Horniman Museum's Accession numbers are given in the Endnotes. I should emphasise that this paper is written primarily to describe the Horniman Collections. The grand topics on which it touches, for example Inner Asian trade, political and religious history etc., are simply outlined as supports or means by which to discuss and contextualise the collections. These subjects are more extensively explored in other literature, such as Basilov, 1989. *Nomads of Eurasia*; Gunder Frank, 1992, *The Centrality of Central Asia*; Sinor 1990. *The Cambridge History of Early Inner Asia* etc.

Nomads - definitions

Given the variety of nomadic societies, generalisations about them are difficult to make (Tapper 1979). As a social type they may be defined by "the co-existence of dependence on livestock with spatial mobility or nomadism" (Dyson-Hudson 1980). The Shorter Oxford Dictionary defines a nomad as, "a member of a people who move from place to place to find pasture" and nomadism as, "leading a roaming or wandering life".[2] One often comes across comments about true nomadism in the literature, in contrast with other forms of pastoralism such as transhumance. These distinctions appear to be based on the romantic desire to define nomadism as perpetual, random wandering by mounted herdsmen.[3] That is, to define true nomadism in spatial, temporal and physical terms. Such cases are rare. Isolated cases may exist today in Tibet and Kyrgyzstan, but these never appear to have been the norm. From the first millennium BC onwards, that is, from the time of the earliest historical records, most nomadic societies held to fairly defined, if varying, pasturelands rather than random wandering. Although major migrations did occur, these were most commonly due to changing political circumstances. In temporal terms, some contemporary nomads, for example Kazakhs in Uzbekistan, some Turks and Kyrgyz, and many Mongols, are perpetual nomads, since members of some families remain as tent dwellers tending flocks on a year round basis. Yet Turks and some Tibetans are pedestrian nomads, and Mongols and Kazakhs were collectivized during this century around fixed settlements, with the effect of constraining their movements.

For theoretical purposes, many Inner and Western Asian nomadic societies must be seen in the context of Russian, Chinese and Ottoman imperialisms, rather than Western European imperialisms. Such an approach is essential in order to counter Eurocentric views which marginalise nomadic peoples and classify them as 'barbarians' (Erturk 1999: 2-4; Sinor 1990: 18). For some 2,000 years, until two to three centuries ago, the nomadic states of Inner Asia had a profound effect on Old World societies and cultures. The development of centralized states such as the Russian, Ottoman and Ch'ing, and their subsequent colonisation of Inner Asia, compounded later by Soviet Russia, fundamentally altered the position of nomadic societies and their relationships with other cultures in this region.

Recent nomadism is perhaps best seen as a variety of adaptive responses to often hostile, settled and ethnically different communities and the state (Bates 1973: 226; Khazanov 1984: 6, 199). Enforced settlement, sedenterization, and in some cases collectivization, have all altered traditional social systems and patterns of land use. I have therefore included within my definition of 'nomadic' societies, those which practise transhumance in varying forms, and I view nomadism as an historical process rather than an example of a pure 'type' society.

Nomadic material culture

Generalisations about nomadic material culture are equally difficult except that there tends to be a weighting towards a number of features which are less emphasised among sedentary cultivators; that is, the need for mobility tends to require portable housing. The nomadic peoples discussed in this paper live in a variety of tents with coverings made of woven cloth and felt. Formerly skins were also used. A major distinction may be made between those peoples who live in felt covered, trellis tents; and those who live in woven cloth, velum tents. This distinction provides a useful analytical framework, but is less clear in some countries such as Iran and Turkey, where both types co-exist. Some nomads have more permanent housing near summer or winter pastures. Mobility is combined with a variety of techniques of animal management and detailed knowledge of types of pasture. In addition, items of diet, clothing and shelter often derive from the products of their herds.

Movement is a key feature in nomadic life. As supplies of water and pasture are exhausted, animals must be moved to fresh sources. Nomads must try to estimate the amount and quality of new pastures, as well as weather conditions, before moving their herds. Migration routes may be horizontal along lowlands; up and down between highlands and lowlands, depending on the different pastures available in winter and summer seasons; or they may circle or radiate from a central place. The nomadic lifestyle is thus a complex relationship between ancient, detailed knowledge about the natural environment: types of pasture, water sources and migratory routes, and contemporary sustainable behaviour.

Animal herds are a desirable commodity. Ever-present threats to nomads are posed by predatory animals, especially to young and weak herd animals; and by neighbouring peoples: rustling and competition for pastures are common. Formerly, nomads were usually armed in order to cope with natural dangers and in their sometimes violent relationships with other groups and societies. Today, nomads have commonly been disarmed by their governments, and they are not usually protected against the ever increasing danger of traffic accidents as road transport across migratory routes steadily increases.

Many nomadic peoples only eat dairy products from their herds rather than meat. Others kill their animals for meat for special occasions, or slaughter stock as winter sets in and provides natural refrigeration. Dairy products, hides and live animals are exchanged with settled peoples for grain, coffee, tea, cloth and other manufactured goods. Many nomads combine herding with some agriculture, and most practice hunting and gathering to supplement their diet.

Western clothing has become common in nomadic societies in recent times, especially among men. Traditional clothing is more usually worn by women. In some societies, for example in Mongolia, traditional dress is again becoming widespread everyday wear, as people seek to express pride in their cultural identity. Nomadic jewellry is made from a variety of materials which may be obtained locally or imported. In some cases traded materials travel immense distances, for example cowrie shells, pearls and coral from the oceans are highly valued and used in central Asia. Jewellry serves as personal adornment, and, as portable wealth, often represents a woman's dowry and indicates social status and group identity. Mens' adornment is often part of functional equipment such as weapons, horses' bridles, bits and stirrups. Jewellry may also be protective. Amulets made from materials as diverse as beads, coins, metal, feathers and mirror cloth, are used to protect both people, especially children, and animals against evil influences.

It is a truism that nomadic peoples usually live in some form of symbiosis with settled peoples, and are dependent on them for the materials and commodities mentioned above. For this reason the material culture of nomads is often difficult to isolate, as a distinct assemblage, from the material culture of their settled neighbours. In terms of their material culture, nomads are usually a part-society. In some societies, for example Tibet, some objects are in common usage among both settled and nomadic sections; this particularly applies to religious material and domestic utensils.

Notes

1. This paper deals only with the Horniman Museum's collections of material from Inner and Western Asian nomadic societies. In general, nomadic material from these regions is poorly represented in ethnographic collections in Britain.

2. Nomads are people who travel to gain their livelihood. The name is often given to people who herd domestic animals, or to people who live by hunting wild game and gathering berries, fruit and roots for food, but it might also be applied to some fishing communities, commuters and labour migrants, Gypsies, travellers and homeless people.

3. The notion of perpetually wandering societies reminds one of the attempt to study pure or isolated tribal societies in earlier anthropology. Yet isolated societies have rarely existed (Wolf 1982), and so cannot be taken as a norm or as typical social forms. Most societies, including nomads, live in a process of development and interchange with their neighbours, which includes aspects of material culture and other cultural traits and religions derived from settled peoples.

Development of Asian Nomadism

Pastoralism is a more recent lifestyle than either hunting or gathering. Pastoralism on a pedestrian basis developed from the mixed economies of cultivating peoples in Western Asia following their domestication of sheep in Iran/Iraq, about 9,000 BC; goats in Iran/Iraq, about 7,500 BC; and cattle in Turkey or Eastern Europe, between 6,000 and 4,000 BC. Mounted herding developed after the domestication of the horse between 4,400 to 3,500 BC in the area of the western (Pontic) steppes of the Ukraine, or in Iran or Turkey; and the domestication of the camel, probably in Turkestan, about 3,000 BC (Heiser 1990: 39, 41, 53, 57).

The domestication of the horse and the development of horse riding, which became widespread on the Pontic Steppes by about 2,500 BC, enabled the peoples there to increase their mobility (Bacon 1954: 44-68; Heiser 1990: 51; James and Thorpe 1996: 51; Ryder 1983: 114).[1] During the 2nd millennium BC, these peoples invented the wheel. Some of the earliest evidence for nomadism in Asia includes rock carvings and remains of ox-drawn covered carts with four disc wheels and canopies, and what appear to have been tents, from the region of the northern Caucasus. Chariots were also developed during the second millennium BC, perhaps also on the western steppes, and their usage spread rapidly: to Egypt by about 2000 BC, and to Anatolia, and China about 1500 BC (Hodges 1970: 75, 139, 231-34; Piggott 1965: 231-234). The use of horses to draw chariots appears to have stimulated breeding methods aimed at producing bigger and stronger horses.[2]

Mounted nomadism provided the mobility and technology necessary to manage a complex collection of different animals: cattle, horses, sheep, goats and camels, which crop and graze in different ways and so may feed on different types of pasture in different localities. *'The ridden horse ... was a "tip over" factor which permitted, for the first time in history, the crystallisation of an Inner Asiatic pastoral nomad way of life.'* (Beardsley 1953: 24-28). The Inner Asian steppes form a *'natural corridor linking ... northern China and the Altai, the southern Urals, Caucasia and the southern Ukraine ... living on these steppes ... called for a highly specialised knowledge of animal husbandry and a notable degree of cultural adaptation ... in riding, clothing and habitation'* (Clark 1961: 166).

Mounted nomads developed social systems which outlasted those of the ancient and classical worlds: commonly, one tribe would become the elite Royal Horde, which ruled other nomads and conquered cultivators, until it was replaced by another more powerful tribe (Basilov 1989; Khazanov 1984). Pressure at any one point, from settled societies or other nomads, often involved sequential displacements of peoples over large distances. These movements have been termed the 'falling domino' effect (Clark ibid).

Mounted nomadism in Inner Asia may be divided into two broad historical periods: from about 1000 BC to AD 1500, a period which was frequently characterised by the formation of nomadic empires; and from about AD 1500 to the present, a period characterised by nomads suffering increasing marginalisation due to imperial expansion.

A significant factor in the new lifestyle of mounted nomadism from its beginnings, was an increased capacity to wage war on settled peoples, especially when horse riding was combined with the use of the composite bow, which was perhaps also invented by the peoples of the western steppes. After the development of mounted nomadism, nomadic peoples, although always in a minority, had an important role in periodically conquering settled peoples and founding large empires, such as those of the Mongols and the Timurids; and in spreading the ideas and technologies of very different cultures along Asian trade routes. The eventual defeat of nomadic societies armed with bows and spears, by settled societies armed with firearms, was one of the most significant and overlooked processes in modern history.

During the first millennium BC the pastoral nomads of central Asia attacked their settled neighbours to the west and south-west in Syria and Mespotamia, southwards in India, and eastwards through central Asia towards China. These peoples, *Indo-Europeans*, were variously known in Western Asia, as Hittites, Cimmerians, Scythians, Medes, Dorians, Thracians, Celts, Germans and Sarmatians. Nomadic peoples mounted attacks on China from about the 9th century BC. After the Turko-Mongol peoples of the Altai region in eastern Inner Asia adopted mounted nomadism, from about 500 BC, they increased their attacks on north-western and northern China, where they were commonly termed *Huns*.

Most historical information about nomads derives from written sources from the countries which were affected by them, such as Greece, Persia and China, and consequently are inevitably biased. Archaeological evidence derived in situ, has been obtained mostly from burials such as at Pazyryk in the Altai, Noin Ula in Mongolia, and Scythian barrows/tombs in south Russia, where there are also remains of settlements. Something of this pastoral nomadic expansion is represented in the Horniman Collections from the southern Russian/Crimea area; western Iran or Luristan; and China.

Scythians in Southern Russia

Scythian remains are a mixture of locally made and imported artefacts, a mixture typical of many nomadic peoples throughout history. The Horniman collection provides a representative sample of Graeco-Scythian grave goods from various sites in South Russia, including Olbia and Kertch, and the Caucasus. It includes vases, a jug, a terracotta figurine, a gold earring, beads, rings, a gilt metal horse's head ornament, and bronze fragments.

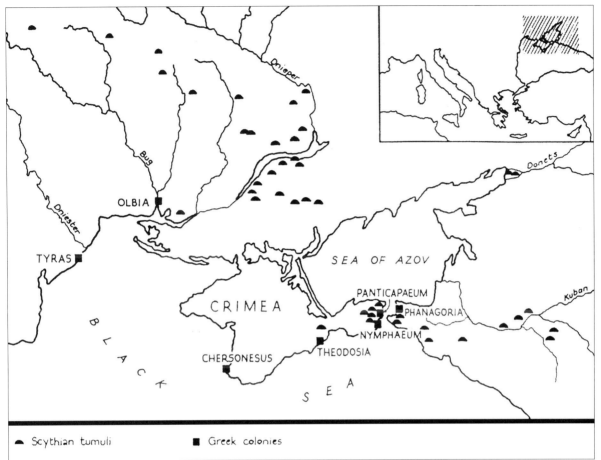

Map: 1
Southern
Russia
(Map: Michael
Vickers, Ashmolean
Museum, Oxford)

▲ Scythian tumuli   ■ Greek colonies

From about 700 BC onwards, Ionian Greeks, mostly from Miletus, began establishing colonies on the northern shores of the Black Sea, primarily to catch, cure and export fish, as well as to gather and export salt, honey and wax, back to Greece. The Greeks quickly established settlements at Olbia, Pantikapion, Tanais and elsewhere which rapidly became prosperous. Here, these settled, literate peoples met nomadic communities already living there – perhaps the earliest recorded colonial encounter with the Other in European history (Ascherson 1995).[3]

The nomads encountered by the Greeks were *Scythians*, cattle herding, horse archers who appeared on the Pontic Steppes after they had been driven from the east, about 750 BC by other nomadic tribes, perhaps Iranian-speaking Sarmatians, who may have moved westwards as the Chou emperors drove away nomads from the north-western borders of China; another example of the domino effect often characterising nomadic movements across Inner Asia.

The Scythians probably displaced the Cimmerians already living in Southern Russia before the 8th century BC, and became concentrated in the southern Ukraine and north of the Crimea.[4] Here they established Royal

19

courts which ruled over settled peoples about 700 BC. Other Scythian tribes moved westwards into Europe and south through the Caucasus into eastern Turkey and Iran, where they allied with the Assyrians, and held a brief rule over the western Iranian border from a kingdom, which was founded about 673 BC on the Moghan steppe in Azerbaijan, until they were defeated by the Medes. After this they returned north to the Pontic Steppes (Crossland 1967: 37-8; Frye 1976: 78-9; Herodotus IV.12; Sinor ibid).

The Greeks of southern Russia lived in 'profitable harmony' with the Scythians, to whom they paid tribute (Clark 1961: 162-3). By 500 BC this relationship included a regular trade in 'barbarians', that is of enslaved captives taken by Scythian chiefs in their own internecine wars, in a 'purely private business carried on by traders who had their (own) personal connections outside the Graeco-Roman world proper'. This trading agreement was purely commercial and had nothing to do with military activity or piracy (Finlay 1972: 162-3).[5]

One of the earliest accounts of central Asian nomads comes from Herodotus (495-425 BC). Book IV of his 'Histories' gives an invaluable description of the peoples of Southern Russia and the Crimca including 'the Scythians (who) neither sow nor plough'. Not strictly true perhaps, since the Scythians as with many nomadic peoples of Inner Asia, combined some cultivation with pastoral nomadism. Although most Scythians remained nomadic and probably lived in felt tents when stationary, and in carts with felt canopies when on the move, some groups in contact with settled Greeks, also settled down in towns in the Ukraine and the Crimea, and adopted agriculture. These settled nomads exchanged Scythian grain grown in the Ukraine for Greek luxury goods which were often deposited as votive or grave goods (Clark 1961: 167; Times Atlas of Archaeology 1996: 160-1). Even so, Scythians were different from Greeks. They drank unadulterated wine, smoked hemp and wore trousers! The Scythian saddle was an innovation in horse management, since it was padded with a defined pommel and cantle, giving greater security than the Mediterranean saddle.

The Scythians reached the height of their power about 300 BC, and then yielded to some extent to the Sarmatians, an Iranian people from the east who appeared in South Russia about 400 BC, and were distinguished by their heavy cavalry armed with lances. These nomadic peoples, along with the Huns in the east, dominated the Inner Asian steppes until the first century AD (Rolle 1989: 14).

The Scythian kings were buried in magnificent royal tombs, which contained Greek gold and silver artifacts: pendants and bracelets showing Mediterranean and Persian influences, with motifs of lion's and bird's heads; made by lost wax casting or stamped sheet techniques. Metalworking formed a particular feature of their culture. Entire cities of artisans were employed by the courts, and metals were obtained from various sources: gold from the Altai, copper from Transcaucasia and iron from the middle Dnieper (Simkin 1968: 4).

Scythian art was distinguished by the Animal Style, with its fantastic motifs of stags (especially), birds of prey, goats and boars, tigers and bears (more common in the east) in joined, reduced, distorted, compound and stylised forms that were used to decorate metalwork made in fairly standardised shapes: belt and clothes' plaques, shield bosses, horse harness; or were used as surface decoration on vessels, along with floral and geometric motifs.[6]

Luristan bronzes in the Horniman collection

The Horniman collection of bronzes from Iran consists of twenty three objects in several categories including weapons: two bronze axe heads and four bronze arrowheads dated from the 1st millennium BC; three spear or arrow heads, and two bronze daggers, un-dated; horse tack: including two bronze horse bits dated to the 1st millennium BC, and horse trappings, un-dated; an ornamental animal figure (perhaps representing a bull), un-dated; and jewellry: two pins, one with a ram's head, dated c. 1200 BC, four bracelets, and two necklets, un-dated. There are also several musical instruments in the collection: including crotal or pellet bells, cymbals and clapper bells.[7]

Iranian culture has been characterised for 3,000 years by a mixture of oasis-style settlements, with nomadic peoples living in between, often in conflict situations: "…one may generally conclude that the areas of Iran occupied by nomads in the recent past were also occupied by nomads in antiquity." (Frye 1976: 11, 14)

Luristan is a mountainous spur reaching westwards from the Zagros mountains overlooking the Mesopotamian plain. Nomads and mountaineers from the refuge areas in the Zagros have repeatedly attacked the lowland cities and settlements throughout history. The lower valleys of the Zagros support the cultivation of wheat, barley, cotton, tobacco and opium, but the summer heat prompts people to adopt nomadism by taking their horse, sheep and goats to high pastures (Frye 1976: 9; Ghirshman 1961: 22).

From about 600 BC, some groups of Iranian-speaking Scythians moved south from the Black Sea Area, fought the Medes (Herodotus I, 15, 103-6; IV, 1, 11-12, 511, 26, 93ff), took service as mercenaries for the Achaemenids (558-330 BC), and settled in Iran among existing mountain tribes in Luristan (Crossland 1967: 37-8; Jettmar 1964: 218).

The material culture of this mixture of peoples, a warrior elite ruling others who were either themselves nomadic or practised transhumance, is characterised by bronzes, and numerous iron objects, most of which have been recovered from tombs, pits closed with stone slabs, or sometimes from a tumulus with a stone circle on it, rather than from settlements.

Luristan bronzes are portable objects which have been interpreted as belonging to this elite. They express the high valuation given to the horse, consisting as they do of horse tack: bridle and harness pieces, bits, rein rings for horses and chariots; as well as weapons: iron and bronze swords, daggers, picks, axes (typically decorated with animal motifs), spear and javelin heads, arrow heads; and decorative objects: pins, belt buckles and plaques, mirrors, and cult or votive objects (Ghirshman 1961: 22, 64-5, 99-112).

Two styles are apparent in Luristan bronzes: an earlier, 'settled' style, and a later 'nomadic' style (which appears to characterise the Horniman Collection). Both styles were made by local craftsmen, and show influences from Mesopotamian and south Iranian prototypes, including a motif of Gilgamesh-style combat; and Scythian style from the Eurasian steppes, seen in animal heads on bracelets, pins and axe heads. Bronze, gold and silver casting was done in open and two-piece moulds and by the lost wax technique; sheet metal was beaten to make vessels. Two chronologies have been proposed for these bronzes: a 'long' chronology (Godard

1958) which dates them from between 1200/1000 to 680 BC; and a 'short' chronology which dates them from the 8th or 7th centuries BC onwards (Ghirshman ibid).

Luristan bronzes began to appear on the market in the 1920s (although the British Museum had acquired one piece in 1854, Moorey [1974, 7]), and were first acquired by European museums in number from 1928 (Frye 1976: 68-70), but their quantity has raised doubts about their authenticity and some museums have refused to acquire them.

China

The nomadic-related material dating from the first millennium BC in the Chinese collection consists almost entirely of weapons: flint and bronze arrowheads in leaf and triangular shapes; a jade arrowhead engraved with symbols; two bronze knives, one with a ring hilt characteristic of those used by the northern border peoples of China and of Siberia; and a bronze sword, dating from the Han Dynasty (206 BC-220 AD). Material from a later date includes trade items such as silks and tea bricks.

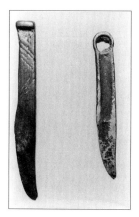
Figure 2: Knife Money, China (Photograph: Horniman Museum)

The dominant influence in the earliest relationships between the nomadic peoples of Inner Asia and China are still contested. In one version, the development of wheeled transport and mounted nomadism on the southern steppes of Russia during the third millennium BC, coupled with bronze working techniques and the use of the composite bow, which was probably invented by the nomadic peoples of Central Asia, diffused eastwards across Inner Asia to China. The earliest development of these techniques in China occurred under the Yang (about 1800 BC) and more particularly under the Shang Dynasty (1500 – 1050 BC). Objects in Animal Style art are also present in the Ordos region of northern China, and the place of origin of this style: China, Siberia or Scythia, is also subject to debate. Some Animal Style motifs, distorted animals, birds and ram's horns, persist to the present day in the decorative arts of Mongolia and Central Asia.

Nomadic peoples to the north and north-west of China became increasingly troublesome to the Chinese, and during the 9th century BC the Chou emperors drove them to the west, which displaced other nomadic peoples across Inner Asia. However, some nomadic societies resisted Chinese pressure and remained a recurrent threat, as well as repeatedly founding dynasties which conquered and ruled China itself. From about 500 BC the Turko-Mongol peoples on the northern borders of China adopted mounted nomadism and the use of the composite bow, probably under the influence of nomads to their west, and increased their attacks upon China.

By the 2nd century BC a confederation of Altaic tribes on the northwestern borders of China, referred to as the 'Hsiung-Nu' or 'Huns' formed the first great nomadic empire which, at its peak, stretched from Zungaria in present day Xinjiang to Korea. The Hsiung Nu controlled the gold route between China and Siberia, and the 'Silk Road' between China and the west. The Chinese allied themselves with other nomadic peoples to the west of the Huns, the Yueh Chi or Sarmatians, but the latter's defeat by the Huns produced another migratory, 'domino' effect among the peoples of central Asia, which eventually resulted in the establishment of nomadic dynasties such as the Kushans.

The Kushan empire (c 100 BC – AD 250), which ruled much of western central Asia and northern India, fostered the spread of Buddhism across central Asia, and, with other nomadic peoples (generically called 'Tartars' by the Chinese) controlled the trade routes which were developing across Asia between China and Rome. Nomadic-ruled states now dominated Inner Asia and peripheral societies including China, Iran and Russia for most of the next 2,000 years. Some of these became well established, for example the Scythian kingdoms in the west and the Hun empire in the east both lasted for several centuries despite reverses. Although the empire of the Huns was broken by the Han Chinese in the 1st century AD, the Hun state remained powerful and stable, and dominated the steppes for another two and a half centuries after 174 BC (Barfield 1989: 36; Bowles 1977: 258; Boyer 1995: 186, 192, 213, 407; Elisseeff 1957: 219-30; Vainshtein 1980: 17-18; Watson 1971).

Notes

1. The teeth of horses from the Copper Age site dated c. 4,000 BC, at Dereivka in the southern Ukraine appear to show traces of wear from rope bits under microscopic analysis (James and Thorpe 1996: 51). The earliest metal bits date from c. 1500 BC. The earliest evidence for horse riding is poor but includes, from c. 1350 BC: paintings from Egyptian tombs and monuments; and a Greek figurine. These show riders sitting on the rump - the 'donkey seat'; and see the relief from South Turkey c. 1000 BC showing a rider with a rudimentary saddle sitting further forward (Hodges 1970: 141, ill. 158).

2. Horses were not used for draft until the 3rd century AD in China, according to Thomas (1979: 24)

3. Ascherson observes that this meeting led to the formulation and recording of the first 'colonial' encounter in European experience and to the various discourses which still remain: what is the difference between 'civilisation' and 'barbarism'? What is cultural identity? Where should its limits and distinctions be drawn? Self criticism is aroused - technical and social sophistication gives both gains and losses: 'natural', spontaneous behaviour is left behind in favour of conscious, rational behaviour. These themes were revived by European expansion in the early modern period.

4. Cimmerian origins and distribution are not known. As a people, the Cimmerians were known both to the Greeks settled in the Crimea and south Russia, and in Anatolia where they invaded the Phyrygian kingdom of King Midas c. 675 BC (Herodotus I.6,15) and settled in Cappadocia (Frye 1976: 78). The name 'Scyth' first appears in Assyrian records as 'Ashguzai' in 681-669 BC (Crossland 1967: 37-8).

5. Scythians also served the Athenians as mercenaries. About 477 BC the Athenians established a police force of 300 Scythian archers, state-owned slaves, who were housed in tents, first in the public square, the Agora, and later in the Acropolis. Their number may have been increased to 1000 over the years, and the force lasted about a century. In 339 BC Philip II of Macedonia (father of Alexander the Great) made a calculated slave raid into the Scythian regions north of the Black Sea in order to fill his treasury. The action was perhaps unusual, but he returned with about 20,000 women and children and treasure (Finlay 1972: 162).

6. The Scythians may have created the Animal Style about 1000 BC, but there is difference of opinion about this, and Siberian

and Chinese origins are also proposed. The Sarmatians developed this style further by using more gems, glass and paste inlays in anecdotal belt plaques and buckles; a popular motif was the Great Hero - an armed rider. Scythian Animal Style influenced Celtic art, for example at Hallstatt and La Tene in eastern and central Europe (Clark 1961: 171; Crossland 1967: 37-8). The Horniman collection of Graeco-Scythian material was made in 1907 and 1908, either by A.C. Haddon or by H.S. Harrison, both then Curators of the Museum. The Horniman Registration numbers are: Greek vases 7.645-8, 7.650-2; Greek objects from various sites 7.654-664; terracotta figure of Demeter 7.668; carnelian seal ring 7.669; grave goods 7.671-5; Greek beads 8.4-5; phalange and two metal rings 8.6; rings and bronze fragment 8.7.

7. The Horniman collection of Luristan bronzes from Iran was made by H.S. Harrison and O. Samson, both Curators of the museum, in 1936, 1952, 1957, 1960, 1961 and 1964. The Horniman Registration numbers are: two bronze axeheads 36.1; 3.7.57/5; four bronze arrowheads 7.6.61/3,5,6; 31.7.61/12; three spear or arrow heads 7.6.61/2, 4; 31.7.61/13; two bronze daggers 7.6.61/1; 8.12.52/1; two bronze horse bits 7.9.60/3; 31.7.61/6; horse trappings 31.7.61/10-11; animal figure 31.7.61/14; two pins 7.6.61/7; 31.7.61/15; four bracelets 3.7.57/3; 31.7.61/7-9; two necklets 3.7.57/2,4; pellet bells M31.7.61/2; M23.1.64/5; cymbals M23.1.64/1-2; clapper bells M23.1.64/3-4. Dr. J. Souchkova of the National Museum Prague examined the Horniman's Luristan collection on 5.6.86, and gave the opinion that all of the pieces she saw date from c. 500 BC – AD 0, except for the armlet 3.7.57/2 which may be pre-500 BC. The necklet 3.7.57/4 is a rare piece to find in museum collections, which tend to consist mostly of horse harness and armlets.

Heyday of the Nomads 0 AD to Present

3

The period from about AD 0–1500 was characterised by repetitive cycles of nomadic imperialism. Empires such as those of the Mongols and the Timurids were immense in scale and had major effects on the history of the entire Old World. The 'Pax Mongolica' of the Yuan (Mongol) Dynasty of China (1271-1368), was a particularly fruitful period for exchanges between Eastern Asia and the West.

The Horniman collection, as is typical of most ethnographic collections, dates from the latter part of this period, that is the later 19th and 20th centuries, rather than earlier historical times. Nevertheless it contains objects which illustrate some of the main activities which occurred in the earlier part of this period. These collections may be sub-divided under the categories of Weapons, Religions, and Transport and Trade: which includes animal trappings, and commodities such as Silk and Tea.[1]

Figure 3:
Turkic Stone,
Western
Mongolia 1992
(Photograph: Ken Teague)

Weapons

Nomadic attacks upon China led the Chinese armies to adopt the use of mounted archers and iron weapons, and to develop the crossbow in self defence (Barfield 1989; Phillips 1965; Rawson 1977; Ryder 1983: 116). The crossbow, invented between the 9th and 5th centuries BC became the standard weapon of Chinese armies for the next 2,000 years. By the Han period (c. 200 BC – AD 200) the Chinese were mass-producing crossbows in their thousands. The Huns were unable to copy or assemble the complex trigger mechanism, nor could they use the bolts, which were usually poisoned, in their longbows. Repeating crossbows were invented in the 11th century AD. In, 'The Collection of the Most Important Military Techniques', published in 1044, it was stated,

Figure 4:
Magazine
Crossbow,
China
(Photograph:
Horniman Museum)

"The crossbow is the strongest weapon of China and what the four kinds of barbarians most fear and obey ... the drill of crossbowmen (in companies) alternately advancing to shoot and retiring to load; this is something which the Huns cannot even face." (Temple 1986: 218-224).

Although they failed to stop the Mongol invasions, repeating crossbows remained in common use in China, particularly around 1600, and were last used about 1895, when they were outmatched by modern firearms. The Inner Asian nomadic weapon *par excellence* was the compound or composite bow made from layers of horn or bamboo or wood and sinew. In some areas these remained in use until the end of the nineteenth century, but were increasingly replaced by firearms. The collection contains two repeating crossbows, several composite bows, arrows, bowcases and a quiver, provenanced as 'Sino-Mongolian', which are probably Manchu (1644 – 1912) rather than nomadic; a modern woman's bow and four target arrows in the Mongolian collection; and two matchlocks, one from Mongolia, the other Tibetan.[2] Nomads often bought their swords from settled peoples, and it is probable that some of the swords in the main Iranian, Turkish and Tibetan collections were once used by nomads.

Nomadic control of Inner Asia ended between the 16th - 19th centuries, when the Russians and Chinese (Manchu) empires expanded onto the steppes and defeated nomads armed with bows and lances by the use of firearms. The end was marked by the Battle of Geok Tepe in 1881, and the final defeat of the Turkomen by the Russians in 1885. This protracted defeat was one of the most important processes in modern history.

Trade and transport

Evidence from the assemblages of grave goods from Scythia to the Altai (Pazyryk) demonstrate that Inner Asia, despite the long distances and difficult terrain, was a region which saw the rapid transmission of

Figure 5:
Camel
Harness,
Yarkand
(Photograph:
Horniman Museum)

technologies such as papermaking, blockprinting and ceramics, ideas and religious beliefs, theatrical techniques and puppetry, and commodities, notably silk and later tea, along the trade routes which crossed it in all directions. The Chinese imported precious materials such as jade[3] from Khotan in Central Asia from the 2nd millennium BC onwards until other deposits elsewhere in China and in Burma, were discovered and exploited during the Ch'ing period (1644-1912).

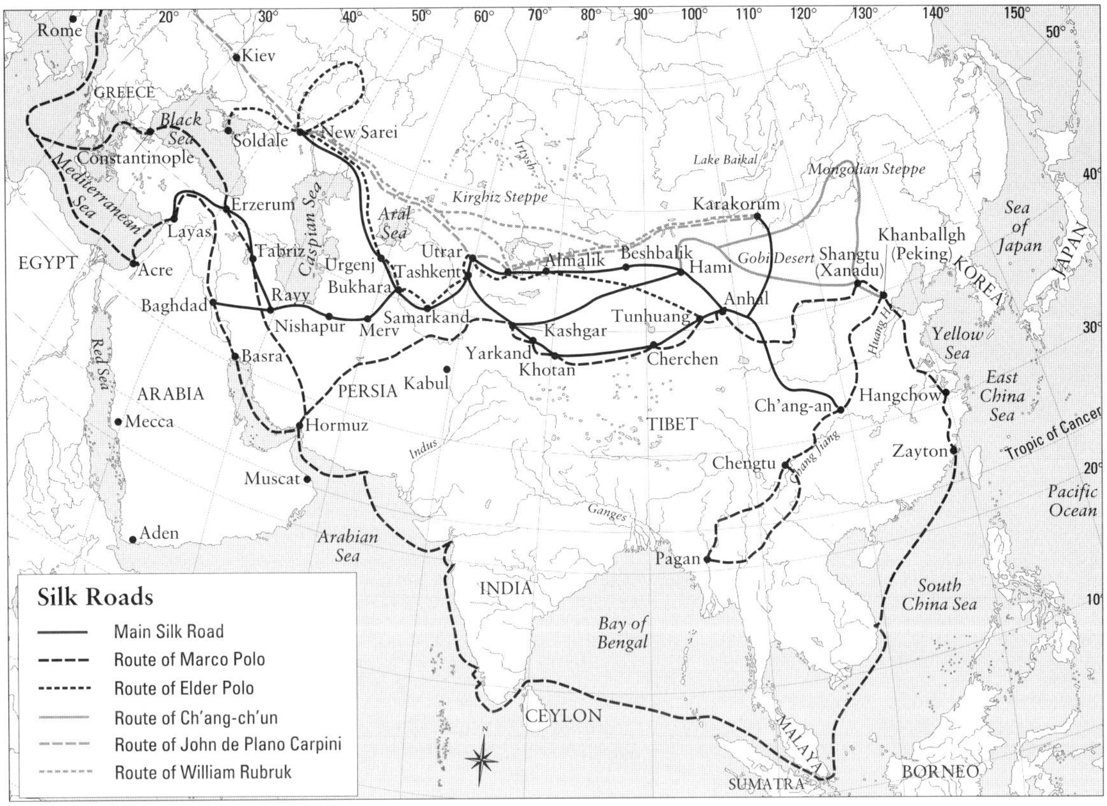

Map 2: Silk
Roads in Asia

The nomadic empires played a key role in safeguarding and promoting trade in exchange for tribute, and provided the animal transport: camels for pack transport, horses for guides and guards, to facilitate trade. In times of political and economic upheaval the nomads turned to raiding the trading caravans and the oasis cities which formed primary staging posts.

Animal transport was essential to these activities. The Horniman collections include horse harness: bridles, bits, saddles, saddle carpets and decorations from a number of countries in Inner Asia: Mongolia, Tibet, Kyrgyzia, Iran (Turkomen), and Turkey. Two pile-woven bags for tent struts, Turkoman, collected by Sir Aurel Stein; and a whip from the Altai are especially notable pieces. Camels, the 'lorries' of the pre-modern age, are still used as transport today, if in decreasing numbers, and are represented in the collection by camel harness from Yarkand, Xinjiang; Iran and Turkey.[4]

Commodity trade – silk and tea

The museum's collections are fragmentary in illustrating the story of silk during these centuries, but are not entirely without interest. They include samples and pictures of sericulture in China; embroidered silk Dragon robes from China, which, although dating from the Manchu period in the 19th century, share features in common with Mongolian robes: cuffs shaped like horse's hoofs and the general cut of a riding robe, indicating nomadic influence. From Central Asia, the collection contains six embroidered caps collected by Sir Aurel

Stein, and a number of samples of modern *ikat* or *atlas* from Margilan in the Fergana Valley. Such material is commonly bought and used by nomadic peoples, including Kazaks and Kyrgyz, to make tent hangings and clothing.[5] Mention should also be made of the Singer sewing machine dating from 1880 which is in the collection. About this time Singer had a large depot in Kyrgyzstan, where their machines were bought by nomads from all over Inner Asia and Siberia (Pahlen 1964: 213).

A note about currency is also relevant in this commercial context. The collection contains three examples of nomadic women's headdresses which use coins or shells as decoration: a Kalmuck hat from the Tekes valley in Xinjiang, a hat from Turkestan, and another from Afghanistan. The Chinese collections contain examples of 'knife' currency, which was commonly used on the northern borders in trade with nomadic peoples.

Chinese silk was apparently traded to the Mediterranean as early as the first millennium BC, and has been found in Egyptian mummy cloth dating from about 1000 BC (Lubec 1993: 25). From about 200 BC, during the Han period (207 BC- AD 220) the Chinese began to develop trade routes, the so-called 'Silk Road', across Inner Asia westwards to the Mediterranean in order to side-step the Hsiung-nu, who had grown wealthy on the silk they exacted as tribute from the Chinese. However this scheme failed and successive nomadic states continued to exact silk in large amounts from the trading caravans which crossed Asia.

The term 'Silk Road' is simply a 19th century European phrase of convenience, which obscures the fact that the routes carried many other commodities apart from silk, including spices, furs, iron and ceramics westwards, and gold, silver, amber, ivory, textiles, and Central Asian horses, the 'celestial or heavenly horses', eastwards (Boulnois 1966: 204; Simkin 1968: 35-6). One main route ran west across China from Xian/Chang'an to Dunhuang, around the Takla Makan desert, through present day Kyrgyzia and Uzbekistan, and Iran to ports on the Mediterranean and the Black Sea. The importance of routes varied according to political circumstances. From the 8th century onwards, Arab pressure forced northern routes above the Caspian Sea to be more commonly used, until southern routes were re-developed during the 16-18th

Figure 6: Right: Teabrick, China
(Photograph: Horniman Museum)

Figure 7: Far right: Samovar, Russia
(Photograph: Horniman Museum)

centuries. This latter period is commonly thought to have seen a decline in Inner Asian trade due to the opening of maritime routes between China and western Europe. Nevertheless, it experienced not only a continuation but an expansion of trade, for example in tea, between China, Mongolia, Russia, and Central Asia, and in horses between Uzbekistan and Iraq to India (Erturk 1999: 1-2; Gunder Frank 1992, 1999: 35).

Nomadic peoples of Inner Asia had a major role in the development of the overland trade in tea, by providing transport, guards and guides, and as consumers. The primary material at the Horniman on this topic is located in the Tibetan and Mongolian collections (discussed below), particularly in their sections on food preparation and utensils.[6]

Chinese tea, transported in the form of bricks of compressed leaf, was traded to Tibet and Turkestan from the 10th century onwards, commonly in exchange for horses from nomadic peoples; and later through Mongolia to Russia during the Ch'ing period. In turn the Russians introduced the samovar to Central Asia in the 19th century, where it was received enthusiastically by the nomadic peoples and is still in use today.

Religions and philosophies

The nomadic peoples of Inner Asia have supported and transmitted numerous religions during the course of history, including Shamanism, Buddhism, Islam, Nestorian Christianity and heresies such as Manichaeism. The collections can only hint at such beliefs and practice.

Many people think that shamanism was the original religion of mankind, which first developed in the Palaeolithic or Stone Age, perhaps in north-eastern Asia. From there it spread to many parts of the world where it incorporated local beliefs and practices, and established new indigenous religions such as Bon in Tibet. A contrary view sees shamanism not as a coherent system of beliefs and practices, but as having developed from folk beliefs following the spread of more formalised religions such as Buddhism and Islam. Shamanism is a particular feature of many nomadic societies in Inner Asia, for example, shamanistic beliefs

Figure 8: Far left:
Obo near Hovd, Western Mongolia 1992
(Photograph: Ken Teague)

Figure 9: Left:
Shaman's Figure, Altai Mountains
(Photograph: Horniman Museum)

Figure 10: The
White Old Man
in celestial
combat,
Mongolia 1979
(Photograph:
Horniman Museum)

and practices are well known to persist in Islamic societies, yet the material evidence from these societies is sparse. This contrasts with the larger amount of material from Buddhist societies.

Figure 11:
Votive ladle,
Mongolia
1979
(Photograph:
Horniman Museum)

Shamanism as it has been observed in recent times, for example in Mongolia, is a means of healing and divination, a means to restore the balance between people and the spirits of the land, that is between the natural world and human society, as well as a method of divining the weather and retrieving lost livestock.

Shamanistic material culture consists of monuments such as sacred mountains and trees, costume and musical instruments. The Horniman collection contains two drums: one from Buriat Mongolia, the other from Tibet; a shaman's figure from the Altai; a wooden ladle for the milk offering from Mongolia; and a number of amulets and talismans from Kyrgyzstan, Uzbekistan, and Turkey. Some of the paintings in the Mongolian collection depict shamanic themes: the journey in the sky and combat with dragons, taming animals and herding deities.[7] Given the preoccupation with animals in shamanic beliefs it is possible that some of the examples of Animal Style art are also of relevance: the 'hungry monster', tao-tieh motif in Tibetan prayer wheels, the ibex on a Mongolian dish, and the birds on Turkomen earrings - vestigial survivals.

Under Communist regimes in the USSR and Mongolia, shamanism was savagely repressed. It is now reviving in Mongolia, but its material culture there remains unobtrusive compared with earlier material from Tuva and Siberia.

The Museum holds a number of examples of Inner Asian Buddhist art and religious apparatus: including thankas and figurative art, particularly from Tibet and Mongolia.[8] It is perhaps not possible to divide these sharply between those objects used by nomadic and settled peoples. The monasteries in these lands served and still do serve as centres which nomadic peoples visit for worship, healing and trade; on a reduced scale in Tibet under the Chinese regime, but on an increasing scale in recently independent Mongolia.

Communism is represented by a fine collection of posters from Uzbekistan and Tajikistan made in the late 1980s. These publicise a variety of topics from space travel to the virtues of bread. Another prize piece is a woven carpet depicting a portrait of Lenin.[9] This genre, which began among the Turkomen, has a defined literature (Dovodov 1983) and provides one of the few samples of pile woven textiles from Central Asia in the collection as a whole.

Notes

1. The nomadic-related material dating from the first millennium BC in the Chinese collection is Registered as follows: flint and bronze arrowheads 27.246-7; 24.7.51/1; jade arrowhead 33.108; two bronze knives NN; bronze sword 24.2.54/3.

2. The later collection of weapons from China is Registered as: two repeating crossbows 818; 7.334; four longbows 5.82; 7.335-

6; 29.167; a whistling or signalling arrow 6.418; a number of other arrows 7.144-6, 7.342, 7.347, 8.7.48/1-9; two bow cases 7.337-8; two quivers 7.341; 29.167; a modern woman's bow and four target arrows 1979.178, Mongolia; two matchlocks 1979.177, Mongolia; NN Tibet.

3. Jade belt buckle, China 9.537; archer's thumb ring, jade, China 33.118.

4. Two pile-woven saddlebags, Turkoman 12.11.54/3-5; a whip, Altai 22.7.48/9; camel harness, Yarkand 27.7.50/4, Iran 1971.660-1, Turkey 1983.43, 1984.73.

5. Samples and pictures of sericulture, China 9.12.53/18-32; silk Dragon robes, China 1970.563, NN773; six embroidered caps, Central Asia 12.11.54/6-11; samples of modern ikat or atlas, Uzbekistan 1998; Singer sewing machine 1996.1; three headdresses, Tekes valley, Xinjiang 27.4.61/103, Turkestan 27.1.60/9, Afghanistan 6.9.52/2; knife currency, China 14.79, 25.210, 24.7.51/1, 15.4.53/1-28.

6. Tea bricks, China 14.74, 1976.81; two Russian samovars 16.55, NN.

7. Two drums: Buriat Mongolia M9.11.50/10, Tibet M2.1988; shaman's figure, Altai 22.7.48/10; votive ladle, Mongolia 1979.184; amulets and talismans, Kyrgyzia, Uzbekistan 1998, Turkey 1973.345-6; 1978.33; 1987.78; paintings, Mongolia 1980.302-5; Tibetan prayer wheel 1973.396); dish, Mongolia 1979.181); Turkomen earrings 16.5.59.. Most shamanistic collections in museums date only from the 19th century. Again the richest collections are in Russian museums, although the Musee de l'Homme, Leipzig, Dresden and Copenhagen also have fine collections. Collections in British museums are small in content by comparison.

8. The Museum holds numerous examples of Buddhist art and religious apparatus, particularly from Tibet and Mongolia (see below).

9. Communist posters from Uzbekistan and Tajikistan 1988.55-71, 1988.111-112, 1988.116-142, 1991.510-17; woven carpet with a portrait of Lenin 1999.15.

Mongolia

The Mongolian collection was acquired from 1948 onwards, and largely consists of recently manufactured material.[1] It numbers about 200 objects, and was assembled during three periods: before 1979: - nine specimens of clothing, dishes, a whip and a shaman's figure; in 1979: - a systematic collection consisting of a tent or *ger*, and its furnishings; objects relating to animal management, clothing, pastimes, paintings and decorative art both for domestic use and as turistica for the Communist bloc; and after 1979: - thirty five objects including currency, textiles and turistica. Despite the relatively small number of specimens this is one of the largest collections of Mongolian material in Britain.

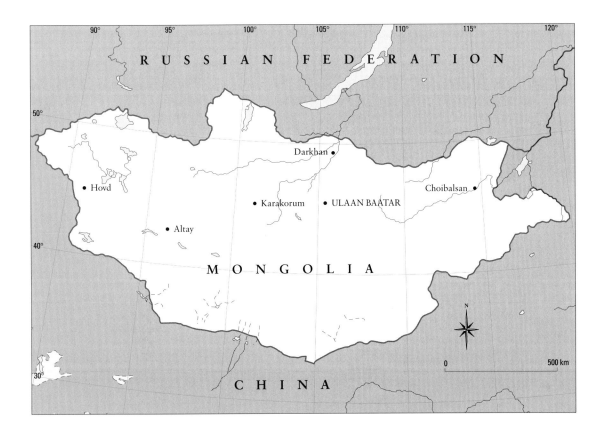

Map 3:
Mongolia

The centrepiece of the 1979 collection is a typical Mongolian tent, *ger*, and its contents. The *ger* consists of a wooden framework: a wooden door and its frame; five, collapsible trellis panels which form the walls; a roof wheel with two supporting pillars; and eighty one roof struts. This structure is enclosed with coverings consisting of an inner lining of coarse, white cotton, two quilted roof covers and a roof-wheel cover, three quilted wall covers, an outer cover of white cotton canvas, an inner cotton lining, a windshield and a lintel decoration, all in dark-blue and red cotton; and binding ropes. All of these components are factory-made, and may be purchased as required on the open market. Formerly the framework of a *ger* was covered with layers of hand-made felt sheets or skins, and the framework and covers secured by ropes made from yak and horse hair. Following Independence in 1991, felt is again being made in rural areas by the traditional technique of dragging it between two horsemen.

The *ger* framework is self-supporting. The roof struts pass upwards from the ears of the trellis walls to sockets in the central roof wheel, which is also supported on two pillars. Five trellis panels provide an average size tent, but eight panel tents are not uncommon and very large tents are used for receptions and public activities.

A *ger* is well insulated, streamlined and portable. The windshield around the base of the walls, can be raised

Figure 12: *Ger* with cheese drying on the roof, Western Mongolia 1992
(Photograph: Ken Teague)

Figure 13: Far left: Milk container, Mongolia 1979

Figure 14: Centre: Tea bowl, detail of base, Mongolia 1979

Figure 15: Left: Dish with Ibex motif, Mongolia 1979
(All Photographs: Horniman Museum)

and the roof flap opened to allow ventilation. A family may use several tents for dwelling, cooking and storage. On more permanent sites, for example in city suburbs, the *ger* may be mounted on a wooden base, with electricity wired in to provide power for lights, refrigerators, radio and television. Formerly elaborate carving and painting of the wooden structure indicated differing social status and wealth, but today they more likely show off the occupant's personal artistic skills.

Inside the *ger*, everyone and everything has its place, and formerly strict, customary rules of etiquette and behaviour were followed (Humphrey 1974; and Appendix, this volume). A guest should approach the *ger* from the right, leave his whip outside, loosen his knife so that it is not immediately to hand, and step over, not on to the threshold. Inside, *gers* are divided into male and female halves, to the left and right respectively on entering the door, and into high and low status halves. Honoured guests and the owner sit in the northern half, furthest from the door, whilst children and small animals may sit near the door.

The structure of a *ger* is closely related to Mongolia's religious history, for example the *ger* is regarded as a model of the universe, the roof represents the sky, and the smoke hole, which may be used to tell the time, is also the passageway by which shamans leave the tent to journey to the spirit world; altar settings may by either Buddhist (traditionally), or, in recent years, secular (Communist) in their nature. Changes in the furnishings of the *ger* clearly indicate social and cultural changes (Humphrey ibid).

The Horniman *ger* is furnished with wardrobes, cupboards, two beds, a wash-stand, a table, four stools, and a stove and pipe made from sheet metal; factory made rugs cover the floor and beds. Additional objects include a saddle, ceramic ornaments, food bowls and cooking utensils. These furnishings are supplemented by wider contextualising material: a sporting bow and arrows, a matchlock etc., clothing, a chess set, and animal management equipment: hide and hair ropes and hobbles, a pole-lasso, a horse scraper, and a dung collecting fork.

The other main section of the Mongolian collection consists of various art objects, primarily paintings,

Figure 16:
Right:
Dappled Horse,
Western
Mongolia 1992
(Photograph: Ken
Teague)

Figure 17: Far
right: 'Milking
Mares'
Mongolia 1979
(Photograph:
Horniman Museum)

Figure 18:
Right:
Horsemen,
Central
Mongolia 1992
(Photograph: Ken
Teague)

folios of prints depicting regional costumes, art motifs etc., decorative ceramics and painted plaster masks used both by Mongolians and sold to tourists. This body of material may be sub-divided along the themes of folk/shamanist art, Buddhist art, ethnographic art, *zurag*, illustrating scenes of nomadic life, and secular art: two lithographs, one of Sukhe Bator, the leader of the Mongolian Revolution, and the other of Natsagdorj, the national poet. Metal objects include two copper plaques in low relief depicting a 'Marco Polo' sheep and an ibex, both in Animal Style; and two teabowls with copper bases in the deep undercutting technique characteristic of Mongolian metalworking.

Mongolians live in several countries including Mongolia (Outer Mongolia), Inner Mongolia (northern

Figure 19:
Street shrine
and Maidar
temple, Ulan
Baatar,
Mongolia
1979
(Photograph: Ken
Teague)

China) and southern Siberia. Mongolia is about the size of western Europe and has a variety of environments ranging from sand and scrub desert, the Gobi, steppe grasslands, and forested hills and mountains in the north. The climate is fairly dry with very cold winters (sometimes -40 C) and short, hot summers when there may also be freezing temperatures and hailstorms. Cultivation is thus severely hampered. Forty per cent of the total population of 2.2 million people still live in tents, and the number may now be rising following Mongolia's independence from the former USSR.

Mongolians herd sheep, goats, cattle and yaks, camels and horses, and, in the north, reindeer. Herding is mostly done from horseback between fairly fixed pastures. Grazing patterns have varied throughout history, today pastures are often centred on a collective settlement. The herds provide for most of the Mongolian diet of meat and dairy products: cheese, yogurt, and milk , which may be fermented to make kumiss, the national drink. Animal products are exported and foodstuffs, rice and tea, and commodities such as silk and synthetic textiles are imported.

The basic unit of society is the joint or extended family For preference a man, his wife and sons, and their wives and children remain together as a camp. Daughters receive their share of family property as dowry when they marry out of this group.

For centuries the Mongols had an important role in trans-Asian trade. Their camels provided transport, and their horses gave them the mobility to serve as guides, guards and raiders on the caravan routes along the Silk

Roads. Mongolian armies repeatedly founded empires stretching across Asia, the best known examples being those of Genghis (Chingis) Khan in the 13th century and of Tamerlaine (Timur) in the 14th century.

In the 13th and 14th centuries the Mongolian empire with its own shamanistic beliefs and practices provided a meeting ground for many religions including various forms of Christianity, popular among the Mongol princesses, and Tibetan Buddhism, which became established as the state religion in the 13th century under Kublai Khan. After their expulsion from China in the 14th century, the Mongols reverted to shamanism, and then were re-converted to Buddhism from the 16th century onwards.

Mongolia fell under Chinese domination during the Ch'ing period (1644-1912). After the Mongolian Revolution of 1921, Outer Mongolia passed from Chinese to Russian control, and, from the 1920s until the early 1990s, was a Communist country (the Mongolian Peoples Republic) and a satellite of the USSR. In the 1930s and 1940s the government followed a Stalinist line which resulted in the repression of shamanism and the decimation of Mongolia's Buddhist monasteries, monks and craftsmen. This destruction of a Buddhist culture, which was comparable with that of Tibet before the Chinese invasion in 1950, had effects on Mongolian material culture which are still apparent in the reduced quality of craftsmanship as is illustrated in the collection.

Recent political changes following independence have affected the economy, and health and social welfare provision have declined. Buddhism is now becoming re-established and traditional medicine is being re-adopted. However, the pastoral herding lifestyle is still essential economically, and is highly regarded and celebrated in painting, sculpture and films.

First hand experience enables me to describe something of the context of collecting in this case. Most of the Mongolian collection was acquired during the period of the 'Cold War'. The Horniman Museum had links with the Communist bloc from 1957, when Otto Samson, the then Curator pioneered collaboration with state museums that resulted in a rich collection of Romanian material culture. These links were strengthened during the 1960s to the 1980s, when the Museum provided a venue from time to time for temporary exhibitions from south-eastern Europe. The Museum, through the backing of the Visiting Arts Unit of the British Council, became the main 'window' for the display of material culture from the Communist world in Britain.

In 1978 the Cultural Agreement between Britain and the Mongolian Peoples Republic was coming to an end with little activity to show for it. The dominance of the USSR on most aspects of Mongolian life and the vagaries of the Cold War rendered cultural relations with Mongolia difficult. Although the Museum had previously made collections of Mongolian musical instruments and sound recordings through its musicologist, Jean Jenkins, it was now felt that an ethnographic collection would fulfil the need for increased cultural exchanges. The Mongolian Artists Union therefore proposed to assemble a collection which would be exhibited at, and subsequently acquired by the Horniman Museum. This offer was accepted, and, in January 1979, as curator for the Asian collections, I was dispatched along the Trans-Siberian railway to Ulaan Baatar to select more objects to complete the collection and to negotiate its purchase.

In considering the objectives in making the Mongolian collection one should distinguish between those of the Mongolians and those of the Museum. In 1979 the Mongolian Peoples Republic was very much in a state of dependency on the USSR and had little representation in the world outside the Communist bloc. Although there was a so-called 'thaw' in East/West relations following Stalin's death, in practice this had little effect. While the Cold War continued the Mongolians refused to permit the necessary fieldwork to acquire contextualising information on the collection. Research was initially restricted to library and archival studies in Britain until several years later.

Despite this, since its formation the Horniman collection has provided one of the major representations of Mongolian society and culture in Britain, and has therefore served the purposes of the Artists Union and the former Mongolian government. An estimated two million people in Britain have seen part or all of this collection during the 1980s and 1990s. For the Museum's part, the presence and display of its Mongolian collections has been a powerful impetus to developing research and interest in this area. Since the collapse of the USSR and Mongolian independence the Mongolians have unearthed and exhibited sumptuous collections of their own material in several countries.

Notes

1. The Mongolian collection consists of about 200 objects: pre-1979 collection: nine items of clothing, dishes, a whip and a shaman's figure 22.7.48/7-10; 7.10.51/12;12.11.54/13; 4.10.61/1; 1972.212, 1972.235; 1979 collection: a tent, *ger*, and its furnishings; objects relating to animal management, clothing, pastimes, paintings and decorative art 1979.2-5, 1979.97; 1979.109-187, 1980.288-311; post-1979 collection: thirty five objects including currency, textiles and turistica 1981.566-571; 1984.77-78; 1988.115; 1989.13; 1990.95-96;1990.201-3; 1992.330-345; 1994.44.

Kazakhs and Kyrgyz

The Horniman's collections from Kazakhstan and Kyrgyzstan are small and serve only a 'linking' function as sample material between Eastern and Central Asia.

Map 4:
Kazakhstan
and
Kyrgyzstan

Kazakhs

The Kazakh collection consists of textiles: a floor felt and embroidered tent hanging collected in western Mongolia in 1992, another embroidered tent hanging, *tus kiis*, and a two men's hats, collected in Almaty in Kazakhstan in 1998.[1]

'Kazakh' originally meant 'nomad, wanderer, freeman, adventurer', or 'steppe rider' (Bowles 1977: 270-1); the latter term was originally applied to them in Turkish records, and adopted from the 16th century by the Russians.

The Kazakhs, a Turko-Mongolian people, were part of the Uzbek nation but broke away from them in the

Figure 20: Right: Kazakh camp, Kyzyl Kum, Uzbekistan 1998

Figure 21: Bottom right: Kazakh yurt and bulldozer, Kyzyl Kum, Uzbekistan 1998

Figure 22: Far right: Kazakh herdsman playing lute, Kyzyl Kum, Uzbekistan 1998

(Photographs this page: Ken Teague)

11th century. At this time the Kazakhs already had their own distinctive economy based on 'tent-wagon' camps, and had a unique, genealogically based, socio-political structure, which had some similarities to the Mongolian form. Although in part sharing a common origin with the Mongols, some Kazakhs living in the Altai still claim descent from Genghis Khan, the Mongols and Kazakhs were traditional enemies.

After the Mongol empire collapsed in the 14th century the Kazakhs formed part of the political confederacy of nomad tribes known as the Golden Horde. They remained nomadic when most of the Uzbeks settled in oasis centres, and often raided Uzbek settlements.

The Kazakhs came under increasing Russian control from 1700 onwards. From the later 19th century, following the Russian conquest and the end of slavery, many former Russian serfs settled in Kazakhstan where they began to farm better irrigated lands. Plough cultivation on pastures blocked nomadic routes as well as preventing access to natural resources.

During the 1920s the Soviets imposed many changes on Kazakh society and culture. They enforced permanent settlement and collectivization of their herds; altered their social structure by abolishing brideprice, *kalym*, and polygamy; and repressed religion - Kazakhs were mostly Sunni Muslims (Pahlen 1964: 59-61). Concurrently enormous mineral resources: copper, zinc, lead, tungsten, gold, tin, and then coal and petroleum, were discovered in Kazakhstan and industrialisation, roads and railways developed. Large scale immigration by Russians, Ukrainians and ethnic Germans followed on as Kazakhstan was turned into a Soviet colony. Many Kazakhs became industrial workers (enforced labour) in Kazakhstan, or became refugees in other countries including China, Uzbekistan and Mongolia where they still live as tent dwelling nomads.

From about 1954 until 1964, large cornfields were created on the steppes by the Russians as part of Khrushchev's 'virgin lands' scheme. Another wave of Russians, Ukrainians and Belorussian workers poured into Kazakhstan. This had disastrous results on local nomadism, and the scheme declined after Khrushchev was deposed.

Today Kazakhs form about 40% of the total population of Kazakhstan, which stretches some 2,000 miles, from the River Volga in the west to the Altai Mountains in the east (one of the largest countries in central Asia). Since independence from the USSR, the Kazakhs claim that they possess a distinctive cultural identity which dates from the 5th century BC, although many are now re-adopting Sunni Islam. In 1998 the children of the respective presidential families of Kazakhstan and Kyrgyzstan were married, perhaps heralding the foundation of a new Central Asian dynasty.

Although some 57% of the total population of Kazakhstan are now urban residents, some Kazakhs still practice nomadism. For example, in 1997 and 1998 I met Kazakhs in the Kyzyl Kum in Uzbekistan who were year-round tent dwellers, tending their family herds, whilst other members of their families were settled in towns; 'authentic nomadism', even though carried out on bounded, fixed pastures.

Kyrgyz

Prior to 1998, the Horniman held very little material from this area: four items of clothing: a fur robe, boots and mittens and a man's hat which was bought in the Grand Bazaar in Istanbul. Given the demise of large-scale nomadism, and the difficulties in collecting in this country, we did not anticipate systematic collecting during our 1998 field season. Nevertheless some interesting material was acquired.

The collection now contains a model yurt and furnishings from Bokanbaev near Lake Issyk Kul.[2] These models are made in various sizes at a local collective, the 'Golden Thimble', for the tourist trade. The Museum's model tent, which measures about 1 metre high by 1 metre in diameter, has 15 struts, a roof wheel, one trellis panel, a door frame with a reed and felt doorflap, a reed wall panel, three felt covers and bands, and

Figure 23:
Family
dismantling
their yurt,
Kyrgyzstan
1998
(Photograph: Ken
Teague)

Figure 24: Far
right: Youth's
cap, Kyrgyzstan
(Photograph: Horniman
Museum)

Figure 25:
Right:
Woman in
traditional
dress,
Bokanbaev,
Kyrgyzstan
1998
(Photograph: Ken
Teague)

Figure 26:
Bottom far
right: Kumiss
flask,
Kyrgyzstan
1998
(Photograph:
Horniman Museum)

a felt wheel flap. The model furnishings made at the same collective, may be combined for display and research purposes with a model man's hat and a model cradle from Osh, in south Kyrgyzstan; and objects from Uzbekistan: two model chests: one from Margilan, the other, inscribed *Cob fa* (Friendship), from Fergana, a miniature Koran stand and model prayer mat, a miniature circumcision, *sunnat*, suit, Fergana, and a costumed doll from Margilan.

The Kyrgyz collection also now includes full-size tent furnishings: four embroidered tent hangings, two felt cushion covers, two felt seat mats, a sheepskin seatmat or pelt rug, a decorative wall panel, a mirror bag, and a red and green floor felt, *shyrdak*, made near Naryn. These provide a mixture of traditional objects, more modern objects made for domestic use, and objects made for the local tourist trade, and commissioned items made for export. The Kyrgyz are reliant on Uzbeks for many craft objects, and a full-size baby's cradle with covers, bedding and wooden spigots for a boy and girl, also reflect the mixture of Kyrgyz and Uzbek items found in Kyrgyz homes.

Men's dress in Kyrgyzstan is now factory-made and European in style, with the exception of the traditional hat, *kalpak*, made in white felt decorated with black embroidery and perhaps velvet. Modern women's dress is represented only by a bride's scarf from Osh Bazaar, but could be supplemented by costume from the collection made in Uzbekistan, which again indicates the interdependence of 'town and tribe'.

Food preparation is represented by two bread stamps from Osh Bazar, a traditional leather kumiss flask from Bokanbaev; and two textile potstands and a potholder from Tamchi.

Figure 27: Saddlebag, Kyrgyzstan 1998 (Photograph: Horniman Museum)

Horses are highly valued by the Kyrgyz, and formerly formed part of the bride price, *kalym*, which was paid in addition to the dowry, and might take years to pay. Kyrgyz sit in a flattened saddle (very different from that used by the Mongolians) which resembles a reindeer saddle (Jankovich 1971: 98-9; Forde 1957: 344-7). The Horniman collection includes a saddle and tack; a whip from Osh; a saddlebag in terme weave; and a saddleblanket used by a rider at the Independence festival held in 1991 to celebrate Manas, the epic hero of the Kyrgyz.

The Kyrgyz are Turkic-Mongol peoples, part of the Altaic language group. Although opinion is divided regarding their origins, they probably originated in the Altai, along the middle and upper River Yenisei in present day southern Siberia and Tuva.[3] In this region, during the 5th to 10th centuries AD, the Kyrgyz practiced a mixed economy based on some irrigation agriculture using a Chinese mould board plough, and stockraising, which was predominant. Pottery, gold, silver and bronze metalwares, which show local Scytho-Siberian, Chinese and Sassanian influences, were well developed (Rice 1965: 53; Belenitsky 1968: ill. 28, 33). Kyrgyz also lived further south, around Lake Issyk Kul, where Buddhist and Nestorian temple/monasteries were built in the 7-8th centuries AD, and eastwards into present-day Mongolia (Mongait 1961: 258ff).

Although they possessed an aristocracy, the Kyrgyz never tried to form a state, unlike some of the other nomadic peoples of this region. From the 9th to 13th centuries the Kyrgyz were successively defeated by neighbouring peoples and were driven out of Mongolia and back to the Yenisei. In the early 13th century the Mongols attacked the Kyrgyz, destroyed their irrigation system and craft production centres, and drove them west and south into their present area in the Tien/Tian Shan and Pamirs, where, during the 16th – 17th centuries, they became squeezed between the Turko-Mongol peoples and the Russians (Barfield 1989: 52, 157, 159,164-5). The Kyrgyz abandoned their traditional shamanistic beliefs and converted to Islam in the late 17th century. However, Islam is not followed in a strict form, and shamanistic survivals such as the veneration of particular bushes and trees, and the use of amulets remain (Smith 1990: 85, 246). Cultural identity is expressed in the epic of the national hero, 'Manas', often performed by traditional bards; in national literature, in the novels of Aitmatov, and in the persistence of expensive and elaborate weddings.

In the Tien Shan some Kyrgyz followed true nomadism on seasonal pastures, without fixed settlements, until about 1900 (Pahlen 1964: 175-6), whilst others practised transhumance between winter settlements and higher pastures (Forde 1957: 328ff).

In the later 19th century, following the tsarist advance into central Asia, the Kyrgyz came under Russian influence. While traditional nomadism persisted, agriculture, mining, trade and urbanisation all began to develop, and Russian colonisation increased during the early 20th century, especially in northern Kyrgyzstan (Bacon 1980: 103). After the Russian Revolution Soviet power was established in Kyrgyzstan in 1919/20. In the 1920s and 1930s the combined effects of collectivization, the repression of tent dwelling and forced settlement largely ended the nomadic lifestyle, although stockraising and transhumance remain important parts of the economy today (Bunn pers comm; Caroe 1967: 144-5; Smith 1990: 246-7).

In 1998 the total population of Kyrgyzstan numbered four to five million; Kyrgyz form over 50%, with Russian, Volga German and Uzbek minorities forming the remaining population. Kyrgyz are also resident in Tajikistan, Uzbekistan, Afghanistan and Xinjiang, with a refugee community near Lake Van in south-east Turkey.

Kyrgyzstan is a high country with two main regions: the Tien Shan mountains in the north, and the Pamirs in the south, which straddle the former Silk Roads between China and the west. The Tien Shan rise to 5-7,000 metres, dissected by river valleys of varying altitudes between, 2,500 – 3,500 metres. Summers are cool and wet, winter is cold with snow. Only 60 days are free from snow, so seasonal activities are marked and most take place in summer. Summer pastures are about an altitude of 3,000 metres. The Pamirs, south-west of the Tien Shan and east of the Fergana valley form a high plateau which is wedged among hills and mountains at an altitude between 300 to 1,700 metres. These have a warmer, drier climate than the Tien Shan.

The major cities of Kyrgyzstan include Bishkek (formerly Frunze) the capital, in the north, and Osh, in the south-west. Apart from industry concentrated around the major cities and towns, the economy is based on agriculture and stockraising. Barley, oats, wheat and millet are grown for human food and animal fodder, but only 7% of land in Kyrgyzia is suitable for cultivation, so most people are involved in stock raising horses, sheep, goats, cattle, yaks and Bactrian camels, by means of transhumance, or 'vertical nomadism' between high pastures, *yaylak* or *jailo'o*, in summer and lowland pastures, *kyshto'o*, near settlements in winter. Pastures are usually clearly defined by tradition as belonging to particular social groups under the leadership of their eldest member (Bacon 1980: 47).

Traditionally, each family had its own set of tents, each woman having a yurt of her own, which were erected and dismantled by the women. Tents were transported on camels and horses, two or three camels, or four horses were needed for each tent and its furnishings. The head of the family lived alone in one tent, the women and children in another. Affluent families owned other, separate tents for guests and the kitchen. Tents are still (1998) in use on summer pastures; beside houses where they are used as extra rooms, to house guests or to hold weddings; and fulfil commercial uses as roadside transport cafes.

The Kyrgyz tent, yurt or kibitka, consists of a willow trellis, four to five feet high, with a separate wooden door frame, and roof struts, curved at the lower end, which pass upwards to a central roof-wheel. This structure is covered with felt sheets and reed walls, chii, (really made from sedge stems not reeds) between the felt and the trellis. The door itself consists of either a felt flap or a reed backed felt flap. The tent is held together with horsehair ropes and decorative woven tent bands. Tent sizes vary, the height ranges from 3 - 4 metres, and the diameter from 4 - 5.6 metres; exceptionally they may have a diameter of 12 metres, and be greater in height.

Tent furnishings consist of textiles: rugs, felts, embroidered hangings and decorative woven bands; as well as painted or leather covered chests, and decorated reed walls, one of which may also be used to separate off a milk storage area; the hearth was formerly an open fire with an iron trivet, but may now be a metal stove. The roof struts and wheel are often stained red in colour. Again, the quality and type of furnishings varies according to affluence, locality and taste. Decorative art motifs, in textiles for example, are the same as those found at Pazyryk, and among the Kazaks (Burkett 1979: 7ff; Mongait 1961: 175; Smith 1990, 249, 252-3).

Notes

1. Kazakh floor felt and embroidered tent hanging, western Mongolia 1992.328-9); three men's hats, Almaty, Kazakhstan 1988. 69-70; embroidered tent hanging, tus kiis, Almaty 1998.

2. Kyrgyz collection: model tent, yurt, and furnishings 1999.12-13, 17, 38-40, 95-6, 101, 108, 110-111, 113-114, 128-129.

3. There are various opinions about Kyrgyz origins. According to Bowles (1977: 362) there is a marked, physical bi-modality between 'Mongoloid' Kirgiz living mostly in tents in the Tien Shan, and 'Europoid' Kirgiz with blonde hair, blue eyes and light skin, who live around the Fergana valley and Issyk Kul area. These latter may represent a Saka incursion into the region. However Kozlov (1988: 25) says that south Siberian features predominate among the Kyrgyz.
Historically, the Kyrgyz are either an offshoot of the Orkhon Turks, from the Orkhon River in what is now Mongolia (Rice 1957: 53), or they claim Mongol origins and descend either from the Yueh Chi - 'felt tent dwellers or nomads', or the Scythian tribe known as Massagetae (Nazaroff 1952: 83-8; 1980, appx); also see Atlas of Man 1981,185; Bowles 1977: 269; Gleason 1997: 43).
Opinions also differ about their name:
a) in Chinese records, where they first appear in the 2nd century AD (SB), they are termed 'Kao-Chu' (Belenitsky 1968: 112)
b) in early Chinese records, the tribes of the Altai region were called 'Hsiung-Nu' or 'nomads'; and then, in the 6th century AD, as 'T'u-chueh', or 'Turk' (Bowles 1977: 258, 262-4).
c) the mountain Kyrgyz are called 'Kipchaks' (Nazaroff 1952: 83-8).
d) in the tsarist period the real Kyrgyz were called 'Kara-Kirgiz', or 'Black Kyrgyz', or 'freebooters' i.e. 'nomads'. by the Russians, and the Kazaks were referrred to as 'Kirgiz' or 'Kaizak-Kirgiz' (Pahlen 1964: 24n). About 1900 Pahlen (1964: 175-6, 215) described the nomadic population of Kyrgyzia as forming three stems: Kara-Kirgiz in the east; Kaisak-Kirgiz or Kazaks in the west, and a third, nameless, stem between them. Their tribal elders were called Manaps or Sultans. Forde (1957: 344-7) observes that the Kyrgyz are closely related to the Kazaks in race, language and way of life. Regarding the Kirgiz-Kazak confusion see Caroe (1967: 85, 105; Smith 1990: 254n 3); and Gleason (1997: 82) on the change of name with independence.

Colour Plate 1:
Kazakh family
displaying one
of their floor
felts, Western
Mongolia
1992
(Photograph: Ken
Teague)

Colour Plate 2:
Embroidery
detail of a tent
hanging,
Kazakh,
Western
Mongolia 1992
(Photograph:
Horniman Museum)

Colour Plate 3:
Embroidery
detail of a tent
hanging,
Kazakh,
Western
Mongolia 1992
(Photograph:
Horniman Museum)

Colour Plates
4, and below
5: Pair of
Saddle carpets,
Eastern Tibet,
1940
(Photograph:
Horniman Museum)

Nomads

Colour Plate 6:
Modern Rug
Belkaya,
Central
Anatolia,
(Photograph:
Horniman Museum)

Colour Plate 7:
Rug Eastern
Anatolia,
(Photograph:
Horniman Museum)

Colour Plate 8:
Rug, Isparta
region,
Western
Anatolia
(Photograph:
Horniman Museum)

Colour Plate 9:
Pair of seat
mats, North
Kyrgyzstan,
(Photograph:
Horniman Museum)

53

Colour Plate 10:
Salt bag, Shah
Sevan, Iran
(Photograph: Horniman
Museum)

Colour Plate 11:
Woman's hat,
Kalmuck; Tekes
Valley, Xinjiang
(Photograph: Horniman
Museum)

Colour Plate 12:
Bag for tent
struts, Uzbek
Lakai,
Afghanistan
(Photograph: Horniman
Museum)

Colour Plate 13:
Pair of bags to
carry tent struts,
Turkomen, Iran;
Sir Aurel Stein
collection
(Photograph: Horniman
Museum)

Colour Plate 14:
Pair of men's
boots, Mongolia
1979
(Photograph: Horniman
Museum)

Nomads

Colour Plate 15:
Beating the
wool to fluff it
before forming
the felt; Western
Mongolia, 1992
(Photograph: Ken
Teague)

Colour Plate 16:
Rolled and tied
felt is solidified
by repeated
dragging by
horsemen.
Western
Mongolia, 1992
(Photograph: Ken Teague)

56

Iran

The collection

One of the Horniman's most notable collections of nomadic material is a felt tent, *alachikh/alacig* and furnishings from the Shah Sevan of north-western Iran.[1] The alachikh is like a flattened hemisphere in shape, about 7 metres in diameter and about 3 metres high. The framework consists of curved wooden struts which radiate to the ground from a central roof-wheel (the Shah Sevan tent is related to Central Asian yurts in its form, in effect this is a 'trellis' tent without trellis walls). The wheel and struts are held under powerful tension by a rope passing from the roof wheel to a large wooden hook anchored to the massive central, wooden tent

Map 5: Shah Sevan, Turkomen, Iran

Figure 28:
Nomad camp,
Shah Sevan,
Mt. Savahan,
Iran; August
1964
(Photograph: R.
Tapper)

Figure 29:
Pitching a
tent, Shah
Sevan, Iran:
May 1966
(Photograph: R.
Tapper)

Figure 30:
Household on
the Move in
the Moghan,
Shah Sevan,
Iran; April
1966
(Photograph: R.
Tapper)

peg. In severe weather conditions ropes may also be passed over the tent and anchored with heavy stones. Screens made of bound canes serve as a wind break around the base of the felt covers, and give privacy in warm weather when the thick felt covers may be rolled up to provide ventilation. The degree of discolouration of the tent felts, which change from white to black with weather and usage, indicates the age of the tent, and so the social status and wealth of the occupants.

The tent forms a single room shared by a family or household, perhaps of seven or eight people, wealthier families may have more than one tent per household. The sunken hearth lined with flat stones, situated between the central tent-peg and the doorway, is the centre of domestic life and represents family unity, whilst specific areas within the tent are allotted to different activities, for example housework to the front, and entertainment and resting to the back. The contents consist of textiles: storage bags, camel harness, some clothing, and pile and flat woven rugs, *kilims*, woven on upright and ground looms; cooking and eating utensils; and carding and spinning equipment. The staple diet is based on wheat bread, which is obtained by trading wool, animals, and dairy products: milk, yogurt, butter and cheese, along with rice, meat, fruit and tea. Food is eaten from a cloth spread on the floor.

At a wedding several tents are used: the groom's father's tent, which serves as a kitchen; the women's guest tent; the bridal tent; the bride's father's tent; and the men's guest tent. The *alachikh* is the central symbol of Shah Sevan cultural identity. However, one in three families cannot afford such a tent and so use simpler forms.

Richard Tapper, a British anthropologist who has done fieldwork among the Shah Sevan, provides a rich source of information (1979) on the *alachikh*: the wooden framework is made by settled specialists, *Tat*, in the towns. In 1966 the wooden structure, which lasts about 20 years, cost £100; the felt covers require about 130 kgs of wool, the clippings from 150 sheep. This wool is taken during the summer shearing, and is made up into felts sheets by itinerant feltmakers. The felts need replacing every three years; and the annual cost of maintaining one *alachikh* is over £12.50 (Tapper 1979: 63, 75).

Amongst the other nomadic peoples of Iran, the collection also includes material from the Turkomen, traditionally trellis/felt tent dwellers, who are discussed more fully in Chapter 7. The collection from the Turkomen in Iran is small and consists of: jewellry: a pair of silver earrings, a silver breast ornament; horse harness of gilded metal inset with carnelians and silver mounts, a whip, and a pair of tent strut bags collected by Sir Aurel Stein; a pair of handcuffs for Iranian slaves, which reflects Turkomen slave-raiding in the 19th century; five modern floor felts from the Yomut Turkomen; and a tent band from the Iran-Russian border, which is probably Karakalpak.

Iran is a plateau, bordered by mountain ranges which rise to 1,000 – 1,700 metres in altitude and run south-east to north west, and across the north below the Caspian Sea. The country has low rainfall, from 120 cms per annum in the south to 240 cms in the north. Vegetation is steppe and desert-like in nature. The settlement pattern is based around oasis towns, which make good returns from irrigation agriculture. The population is primarily settled, but includes some nomads. Both share an 'oasis' ethos, with allegiance given to family and ethnic or tribal grouping rather than to central government or to the nation. The settled Iranians are Shi'a Muslims, but the minority, peripheral tribal groups are often Sunni.

Several nomadic peoples live along the western border of Iran, including Bakhtiari, Basseri, Qashqai, northern Lurs and Kurds (now mostly settled), as well as the Shah Sevan. At the turn of the century nomadic peoples formed about 1/3 of the total population of Iran and frequently raided settled peoples, until the military regime of Reza Shah (1925-1941) suppressed such activity in the 1920s. It also promoted the adoption of European dress among the upper social classes, and dissuaded nomadic peoples from practising migration with their herds. Nomadic numbers dropped to about 1/4 of the total population, and continued to drop until the 1970s, after which there was some re-adoption of nomadic lifestyles.

The primary pattern of nomadism in Iran is transhumance along fixed migration routes between mountain pastures in summer and lowland winter villages where a mixture of pasturage and cultivation is practised. Migration routes may be lengthy, over 100 kms or so. Nomads are a part society dependent on towns and urban craftsmen for cloth, agricultural and industrial products, which are obtained by trade.

Figure 31: Silver earrings with a protective motif of birds, Turkomen, Iran (Photograph: Horniman Museum)

'Shah Sevan' means 'those who love the Shah'. Although this title dates from the 16th century, they were probably not defined as a group until about 1600 and did not form a tribal confederation until about 1740. They are a political rather than an ethnic group. (Tapper 1979). The Shah Sevan live on the borderlands of north-western Iran and Azerbaijan. In the early 19th century the Shah Sevan included 30-40 recognised tribes in two main divisions: the Meshkin, numbering about 6-7,000 members who crossed the Azerbaijan border to the lower Lor River on the Mughan steppe for winter pastures and were more prosperous than the Ardabil tribes who numbered c. 5,000 in the early 19th century, and were mostly settled cultivators whose leaders controlled Ardabil until 1808.

The Meshkin traditionally migrated between summer pastures in Iran and northwards across the border to winter on the Mughan/Moghan steppe in Azerbaijan. The 1828 Treaty of Torkmanchay between Iran and Russia left the Shah Sevan with only restricted pastures on what then became the Russian-controlled Mughan. In 1884 the Russians closed this border to the Shah Sevan, and unrest and banditry followed on the Iranian side. In 1909 the Shah Sevan, in coalition with other local tribes, plundered Ardabil and controlled its region until 1923 when they were pacified and disarmed by Reza Shah. Traditional dress was forbidden in favour of European clothing, young men were conscripted, and many nomads became settled cultivators. In the 1930s migrations were banned and tents were outlawed with disastrous effects on local peoples and their herds. During the World War II period the Shah Sevan resumed nomadism as Iran's central government fell from power. After the war the Iranian administration recovered and reduced the power of local chiefs. By the 1960s the Meshkin numbered about 40,000, and the total Shah Sevan population about 150,000. Along with other nomadic peoples in Iran, the Sha Sevan suffered further difficulties under the Khomeini regime, but again returned to nomadism in the late 1970s. Since then they have again fallen under government pressure to settle.

The Meshkin Shah Sevan keep mixed herds and flocks of sheep, goats, camels, donkeys and horses, cattle, dogs, cats and chickens. Each household has three or four camels; goats form 15-20% of all flocks, the poorer the family the more goats are kept. Goats form 30% of the flocks of poor people, and less than 5% of the flocks of the rich. Goats are tended by women and children, and provide meat, skins, hair and milk; a few billies are kept to lead the sheep (Tapper 1979: 63). The Shah Sevan claim that a herd above 300-400 becomes too large for one shepherd to manage, especially in the mountains, and prefer an optimum number of 200-300. This amount is lower than that preferred in some other pastoralist groups, for example 300-400 among the Basseri, and 500-600 among the Durrani Pashtuns. Settled Shah Sevan now send flocks to summer pastures with shepherds, who have only slings and staves as protective weapons (Tapper 1979: 94, 102, 291n2). The ideal camp should be contained in a circular area with a maximum radius of about 8 km – the distance that a herd of sheep can cover, out and back, in a day's grazing. Summer herding groups consist of four or five tents, winter camps, *oba*, consist of ten to fifteen. On the summer pastures tents may be moved several times over large areas.

The transhumance pattern covers several routes, *elyolu*, which extend over 150 kms in length, and are followed during each spring and autumn. Winter pastures, *qislaq*, are on the Mughan steppe which is nearly at sea level and straddles the Iran-Russian border of Azerbaijan. In spring the animals are moved southwards through spring quarters, *yazlaq*, to summer pastures, *yaylaq*, which rise up to 4000m in altitude in the Savalan Mountains in Iran. This migration may take up to 25 days each May and October.

A migration groups consists of two or more winter camps under the direction of an Elder (Tapper 1979:

39, 93). Traditionally, heavy baggage including the tent was carried on camels, but may now be sent by truck. During the spring migration overnight shelters consist of windbreaks formed from a few of the tent struts, felts and rugs. In the 1960s about half of the Meshkin Shah Sevan (more than 20,000 people) lived in tent camps throughout the year; and over half practised irrigation agriculture.

Notes

1. Shah Sevan collection consists of a tent, alachikh/alacig, and furnishings 1971.67-121, 1975.225-229. The Iranian Turkomen collection: a pair of silver earrings 16.5.59; a silver breast ornament 25.1.61/1; horse harness and a whip 1972.274-5; a pair of tent strutbags 12.11.54/2-4; a pair of handcuffs 27.4.61/66; a tent band from the Iran-Russian border 1971.343 and five floor felts, Yomut 1983.37-41.

Turkey; Linking Collections

The collection

Turkish material formed part of Frederick Horniman's founding collection dating from the 19th century, which has been substantially augmented from 1948 to the present. Much of the earlier collection probably had an urban provenance. Although specific details were not recorded for most of the pieces, some of this material: smoking pipes, weapons, coffee making utensils, amulets, clothing, animal trappings etc., could also have been used by nomadic peoples.

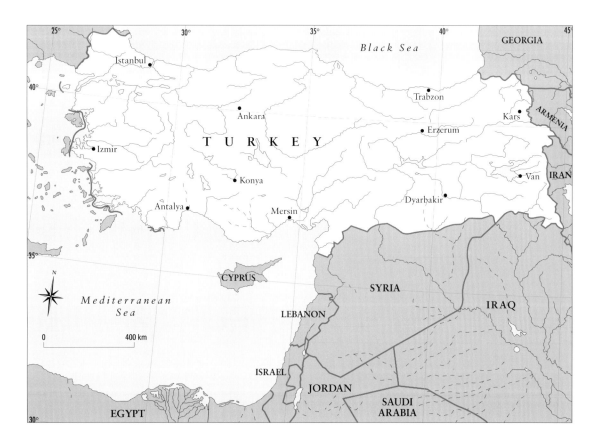

Map 6: Turkey

Particular objects which are most likely to have been nomadic in provenance include a leather water bottle, a donkey saddle and girth, saddlebags, a Kurdish man's cap, and a Kurdish bag and bracelet. It is also possible that some objects in the archaeological section of the Turkish collection are nomad- related: a bronze axehead and a floor felt sample from Beycesultan, both dated to the 2nd millennium BC.

Specifically provenanced nomadic objects includes material in three collections: Brown 1981; Burkett 1983-4; and Teague 1991, 1994 and 1995.

In 1981 a collection of weaving equipment and products from central Anatolia and the Taurus/Toros mountains was made for the museum by the anthropologist Jean Brown, This collection primarily derives from settled villagers, but contains objects made and in use by semi-nomadic Yoruk, who could equally well have acquired and used the village material. These Yoruk lived on the coast at Gazi Pasa near Antalya in the winter, and on summer pastures around Kirobasi in the Taurus mountains in summer. The objects woven by them are two large storage sacks, *cuval*, which are placed around the inside edge of the tent; a cover, *ortu*; and 'pillow', *yastik*, for a divan. The overlapping nature of nomadic/settled material is also exemplified by the Steel collection of pottery, made in the late 1960s, by former nomads settled in north-western Turkey. This collection consists of 276 items of pottery which are made by the women of the settlement, fired by the entire community, and taken for market sale by the men.[1]

Figure 32:
Black tent,
Toros
Mountains,
Turkey 1994
(Photograph: Ken
Teague)

In 1983-4 the Mary Burkett collection, which was compiled from 1962 onwards (Burkett 1979) was acquired by the museum. The Turkish nomadic objects in this collection includes woven and felt objects: three women's woollen cloths, three hats and a hood, four shepherds' capes, *kepenek*, a pair of insoles, a bag, a charm, two floor felts, two camel's headdresses (one is Kurdish and was used on festive occasions), a donkey or horse band, and two breech straps.

The 'Tents' exhibition at the Horniman in 1985 prompted a carpet dealer in Konya, in central Anatolia, to approach the museum with the offer of a collection of tents and their furnishings. In response, I visited central and southern Anatolia in 1991, 1993 and 1994 and made collections of tents: three yurts from Salur Turkomen of the Karapinar region of central Anatolia, dating from around the last 30-40 years, and a black tent from Yoruk in the Taurus/Toros Mountains; tent furnishings: flat and pile woven textiles, including two

Figure 33: Above: Kitchen area, 'stone tent', near Mut Southern Anatolia 1994
(Photograph: Ken Teague)

Figure 34: Above right: 'Stone tent' near Mut, Southern Anatolia 1994
(Photograph: Ken Teague)

Figure 35: Right: Interior of 'stone tent' near Mut, Southern Anatolia 1994
(Photograph: Ken Teague)

tulu rugs; felt rugs and hangings, domestic utensils, cradles, clothing and a saddle and other animal trappings.

The traditional Turkish yurt, *topak ev*, follows the typical Central Asian form. It is shaped as a domed cylinder with a roof wheel, curved roof struts, and a trellis wall with a doorway. This structure is covered with felt sheets held in place with ropes and decorative woven bands. People who can afford to do so often have one tent for domestic activities, carried out by the women in some seclusion following Islamic precepts, and another tent for receiving guests and for the men of the family to sleep in. Tents are also erected alongside a permanent house to serve as a summer dwelling.

The museum's black tent, *chadar/cadir*, was used by Yomut Turkomen in the Isparta-Adanya area in the Toros mountains in southern Anatolia. The coverings of black tents are made from loosely woven goat hair, although camel hair and sheep's wool may also be added. The size and shape of these tents may be varied, depending on whether they are for winter or summer use, by the addition or subtraction of supporting poles. The Museum's version, which has reed wall panels enabling it to be used in winter, is a three-pole tent; the longest central pole, which symbolises both the husband of the family and the core or middle class of society, may bear a talisman as well as other amulets against the evil eye which may be strung between the poles. Black tents, are still used by a number of peoples in Turkey, including Yoruk, Kurds and Yomut Turkomen, primarily in the Taurus/Toros mountains and in eastern Turkey between Mersin and Lake Van.

A number of other types of tents are also used in Turkey, for example, 'stone' tents, *sayvant*, which consist of a wall of uncemented stones from two to four feet in height, which are left on the high pastures from one year to the next and mark the summer camp site. On arrival in late spring, a canopy of black cloth or other textile material is stretched across these walls on a framework of wooden struts to make the summer residence. Increasingly other forms of tents are in use including tent covers made of thick plastic sheeting, or bell and rectangular canvas tents in European forms which are made to order in the bazaar. Kurds, and some Yoruk, also use tents, *mal cadiri*, to house stock during winter. These have many poles and the tent canvas is bought in town and made up to nomad specifications (Bates 1973).

Tent furnishings are mostly interchangeable and usable in all types of tents: pile and flat-woven carpets, blankets, saddlebags and animal harness are all made from sheep's wool, perhaps with goats' hair added; felts are used as floor coverings and wall hangings, and areas for different activities may be defined by stacking storage bags containing food, clothing and other belongings. In winter felts and bags are stacked against the wicker screens for greater warmth.

Among the furnishings acquired in 1991 and 1994 are two *tuylu/tulu*, which may show an intermediate stage between flat and pile weaving, and several pile-woven rugs of some age. The patterns and motifs are not particularly easy to determine. Clear provenances for Turkish nomadic textiles may no longer be possible given the history of social changes which have taken place among these peoples (Landreau 1978: 11-12); but several appear to be from eastern Turkey, the Caucasus and Azerbaijan. A particularly interesting pile carpet, woven primarily for sale or export by settled nomads, Salur Turkomen of Belkaya Kasabasi in central Anatolia, retains Azeri motifs, as do some of the older woven textiles formerly used by these people in this area.

The Museum's collections are particularly rich in felts. The origins of felt-making are obscure, some evidence suggests it may have been in Turkey. Burkett (1979: 8ff) notes that some recent designs in felt are identical to those found at Catal Huyuk in central Anatolia, in levels dating from the sixth millennium BC. onwards. The felt fragment from Beycesultan in the Horniman collection dates from about 2,000 BC. Felt was used for tent covers, and is still made for floor coverings, prayer rugs, clothing: for example shepherds's cloaks, and notably for dervish's hats; and saddlecloths and padding. The collection contains examples of all of these, as well as a fine tent hanging made by refugees (now settled) from Circassia/Cerkes in the 19th century, which patriotically depicts the Turkish emblem, the crescent and star, over a tree of life. Felt making in recent times has been done on a household basis, by treading or 'dancing' the felt by men (Burkett idem), or by the Middle Eastern method of compressing the felt with the forearms, and by machinery in small factory/workshops.

Woven textile production may have been introduced into Turkey by the Turkic peoples. Traditionally women do all their textile production in the home - carding, spinning, dyeing and weaving, when other domestic duties allow. There is little tribal weaving now (Thompson, 1986: 16), although some Yoruk still weave on narrow and broad looms in the summer camps, to make textiles such as *cicim* for domestic use, that is as floor coverings for their tents (Brown 1981). Village carpet weaving traditions remain strong or have been re-developed in some areas, for example in the northwest in Cannakale province, where the use of natural dyes in rug weaving is being encouraged in the Dobag project, around Bergama, in Balikesir, around Konya and Karapinar in central Anatolia, and among the Kurds around Lake Van. Most rugs are now woven as a cottage industry and by co-operatives in small factories, for sale to domestic and tourist markets and for export.

Animal trappings in the collection include a mixture of woven and felt objects for horses, camels, and donkeys: three saddlebags, a felt band padding for horse harness, from Adiyaman in 1978, two felt breech straps: one from Trabzon in 1977, the other from Adiyaman 1978; horse trappings and decorations; two camels' headdresses, one from Cerkan; and one, Kurdish from the Cilo Mountains, dated c. 1940; a donkey's nosebag, a donkey's charm against the evil eye; a decorative band; a felt saddle blanket, and a horsehair girth strap, all Yoruk; near Fethiye, south-west Turkey 1994.

Nomadic peoples in Turkey formerly lived in both the main tent types: felt/trellis tents, yurts, derived in origin from central Asia; and velum or membrane tents, usually made from woven goat hair, (called black tents for convenience) and originally derived from Arabia. Formerly both Turkomen and Kurds lived in yurts and in black tents, without a strict correlation between peoples and tent types. In recent times Kurds mostly live in black tents, and the Turkomen who use black tents in the Toros now tend to buy them from Kurds.

In Turkey the common word for 'nomad' is *Gochebe*, from *gochmek*, 'to migrate', but some of the Turkomen and Kurdish tribes have been called Yoruk, from the Turkish word, yurumek, 'to walk' (Landreau 1978: 11). The aristocracy of the Oghuz tribes who arrived in Turkey in the 11th century believed that their true identity as Turkomen was embodied in their nomadic lifestyle and despised those Turkomen who settled or semi-settled and thereby betrayed their identity. This aristocracy therefore took the name 'Yoruk' to distinguish themselves from settled Turkmen (Khazanov 1984: 266). Yoruk now applies to a number of tribal groups including Turkomen, Kurds and Tatars; and has the connotation of semi-nomads, 'those who walk,' who practice transhumance between winter settlements and summer pastures (Bates 1973: 116).[2]

Turkomen[3]
The Turkomen of Turkey represent the furthest movement westwards of the Turko-Mongolian, Altaic peoples originally from the region of southern Siberia and western Mongolia. These peoples, nomadic, felt tent dwellers whose earliest records and inscriptions date from about the 6th - 8th centuries AD, migrated westwards from the 9-10th centuries, some settling in Afghanistan and Iran en route and converting to Islam, some fighting the Byzantines and Crusaders, and conquering Turkey between the 11th and 15th centuries. The Turkish entry into Anatolia on a permanent basis is marked by the Battle of Manzikert in 1071, when Alp Arslan defeated the Byzantines. From the 1290s onwards the Osmanli family founded a dynasty, the Ottomans, who established an empire which covered much of the Near East and the Balkans until 1920 -21.

The Turks formerly herded sheep, goats, cattle, donkeys camels and horses. Although these animals are still herded today, many Turks settled as farmers during their westwards migration. Several governments from the Seljuks (11-13th centuries) onwards have encouraged the Turkomen to settle. When settled, Turkomen often adopted Sunni Islam, whilst nomadic Turkomen often hold a mixture of Sunni, Shi'a and pagan or shamanistic beliefs.

In the early 18th century the Ottoman government conquered and enforced nomadic peoples in southeast Turkey to settle near their winter quarters. In many cases this was a failure and nomads were re-settled on lower ground or in Syria and Iraq (Eberhard 1953: 49ff). In the 19th century the Ottoman government further sedentarised Turkey's nomadic populations. For example, about 1900, nomads in western Anatolia were given plots of land to encourage them to become settled cultivators (Kandiyoti 1975: 207). Sedentarization continued in the 1920s under the Republic, a process which was occurring at the same time in Iran and Soviet Russia.

These measures led to overgrazing on restricted pastures, an ecological disaster. Many nomads took up agriculture; a scratch plough, ox-yokes, threshing board and rakes in the collections represent this social change.[4] Whilst wealthier nomads could acquire land and become sedentary, many others were too poor to do so, and became the lowest strata of Turkish society who regarded settled life as a form of slavery; many of those who have settled only recently still regard themselves as nomads (Eberhard 1953: 61; Khazanov 1984: 219, 221, 267; Thompson 1986: 16).

Yoruk

The Turkish black tent derives from the Islamic expansion from Arabia in the 7th century AD, and the Arab attack on Byzantium. Historically it therefore precedes the introduction of the trellis tent by the Seljuk Turks in the 11th century. The Muslims were driven back to the Taurus mountains, which became a fluctuant frontier zone. Khazanov (1984: 104) states that the Bedouin could not settle on the Anatolian plateau which was too cold for their dromedaries, but that the Turks with their horses and Bactrian camels were used to the cold and did settle there.

The Yoruk/Yuruk are one of the largest pastoral, tribal groups remaining in Turkey. They were formerly distributed across the entire country, and spoke various dialects of Turkish. 'Yoruk' now appears to be a generic term. Some were named for the distinctive colour of their flocks, the White Sheep People, or the People of the Black Goats. Under the Ottomans, each tribe had a chief responsible directly to central government. They paid pastoral dues, fleeces at the end of summer grazing, and sometimes cash to the local governor, and were liable for military service and corvee labour: building roads, caravanserais and religious buildings, digging ditches and canals, transporting food and arms, cutting wood, charcoal burning and casting cannon (Lewis 1971: 34, 173-6, 191).

The Yoruk tribes were polygamous, marriage was usually within the tribe, although brides might be stolen from others, and weddings were a simple matter involving the exchange of handkerchiefs and a feast. A bride, *gelin*, is distinguished by her cloth headdress with a gold headband, and the locks of her hair in front of her ears. When moving to summer pastures, the string of household camels would be led by a 'fresh', or recent bride dressed in her best clothes and gold jewellry, otherwise the camels were led by a virgin daughter (Bates idem). Women had fairly high status and went unveiled. Formerly each wife had her own goathair tent and followed her own occupation: some herded sheep and goats, some herded camels, and perhaps a few cows, one fetched food and water, one made butter and cheese, one did the weaving. Khazanov (1984: 184), observes that the small-scale, kin-based camps now found are a sign of the recent atomisation of Yoruk society.

Infant mortality was high, and circumcision was practised. This was done by an outsider, sometimes a Jew. A Muslim *hoja* was then invited to the circumcision celebrations some days later and was given a token payment as if he had performed the circumcision. Shamanistic beliefs are indicated by the glass beads which are sewn onto childrens' clothing to protect them against the evil eye, and by the practices of tying cloth strips, or wooden spoons and adding stones near particular sacred trees or bushes where people were buried,

Yoruk are semi-sedentary in winter, when they may live in tents, reed huts, or now in permanent houses. on low-lying pastures, often on the coast. In late spring they move to higher, inland summer pastures. The men lead with the flocks and herds and the women follow with baggage animals. Each family has two to eight camels which are used only for transporting household goods, but not for milking and riding. When moving the women usually load and unload the tents and belongings (one tent forms a camel's load), but increasingly these, along with water supplies, are now carried on lorries and trailers when they can be afforded.

Since the Ottoman period onwards, the Yoruk, when migrating, are never allowed to stay in one place more than three days, nor to damage property. Their movements and behaviour are subject to police scrutiny and punishment. Villagers may also charge fees for passage (Bates 1973: 147). Movement between summer and winter pastures is becoming increasingly difficult as more land is brought under cultivation.

Yoruk diet is frugal, although standards of hospitality to guests are high, and consists of milk products and bread as staples; wheat, rice, dried fruit, tobacco and tea are bought in the towns. Cooking is done on metal plates over a dung fire. Furniture is simple and portable: a loom, woven textiles, bags, kilims and felts, a few utensils and a goatskin churn to make butter, mattresses and saddles. Spinning, to prepare thread for weaving, is done at any time whilst walking or tending animals.

Kurds

Nomadic Kurdish tribes typically live in black tents in south-eastern Turkey. Formerly they migrated between the highlands of Turkey and Iran and the plains of Iraq. This straddling of political boundaries has frequently led to difficulties which continue today. In 1876-7 Frederick Burnaby (1985: 228-9n) on his ride through Anatolia, reported that the Kurds in the Lake Van region of eastern Turkey were in the pay of the Russians, and were being encouraged by them to cross the Russian/Turkish border as Russian subjects without paying taxes to the Turkish Government. Since they were a migratory people, the Russians argued that the Kurds needed to cross the border freely in order to graze their cattle. Burnaby quotes an earlier report that both Russians and Turks were intent on scattering and weakening the Kurdish tribes, and that Russia was doing exactly the same with regard to the Turkomen east of the Caspian, that is, pretending friendship but encouraging neighbouring governments (in the latter case the Shah of Persia), to attack nomads, and so pave the way for Russian dominium. The Ottomans similarly used the Kurds against the Persians.

Under the Ottomans, the numerous tribes of nomadic Kurds were taxed by tent households, each tent contained between five to twenty people. The men tended the flocks, which were mostly sheep and cattle, and moved them between watered pastures (Lewis 1971: 186-7). During migration the unveiled and relatively emancipated women followed with their baggage on bullocks, making their own camps on the way. Women chose their own husbands and eloped if necessary. Betrothal was celebrated at a feast where a brother or near male relative represented the groom, and was followed by a wedding dance attended by as many of the tribe as possible. This was regarded as a binding marriage, monogamy was the custom and divorce was rare. Women managed all duties other than herding, including making dairy products, and managing the family's financial affairs, such as the payment of taxes.

A few Kurds were settled in small towns which served as markets for the nomadic Kurds. The flat-roofed houses were made of sun-dried bricks covered with a mud and straw plaster, with reeds and earth for the roof. Settled Kurds tended to be more law abiding than the nomads, and exchanged a verbal contract before the *imam* when getting married.

Along with the other tribal peoples of the Ottoman Empire, the nomadic Kurds of eastern Turkey and Iraq regarded themselves as autonomous and gave allegiance to their tribal chiefs rather than the central Turkish government. The latter tended only to collect taxes rather than enforcing law and order, allowing the Kurds to engage in their own feuds and factionalism, with illegally obtained firearms, mediated only by tribal justice (Lewis 1971: 190ff).

Sedentarisation was enforced on the Kurds in the 19th and 20th centuries, which led to several uprisings. Most Kurds are now settled agriculturalists and the Turks tend to refer to them as 'mountain Turks', rather than as a separate ethnic group. Political difficulties between the two groups currently continue.

Today, animal husbandry in Turkey forms 30-35% of agricultural production, on grazing lands which still cover 24,000 hectares, almost equal to the land area under cultivation. Stockraising is usually combined with vegetable cultivation. Meat production, the weaving, clothing and leather working industries are among those which are most developed and serve both domestic and export markets (DGPI 1993: 96, 103-4, 106, 114).

Despite this there is pressure on pastures in the southeast, where pastoralists cannot compete with mechanised cultivators and winter pastures have been diminished in size, which results in declining nutrition for the stock leading to a decline in the quality of dairy products and wool (Eberhard 1953: 61-3; Tuncdelik 1963/4: 58ff).

Most former nomads now practice transhumance between permanent winter quarters, and summer pastures, *yayla*, which are rented from those villages and towns that own them as collective property. *Yayla* are variably found in different physical environments including arid/desert regions such as the Konya plain, where 'horizontal' nomadism may be practised onto pastures adjacent to settlements; in the forests of the eastern

Black Sea coast; and in the mountains above the tree line, in the Taurus mountains, eastern Anatolia, and the Black Sea mountains (Tuncdelik 1963/4: 58ff).

Figure 36: Shepherd in a felt cloak, Central Anatolia 1994 (Photograph: Ken Teague)

A common pattern among black tent dwellers is to spend winter in lowland camp groups consisting of two to five tents near the sea, where they may do some cultivation or work as casual labour, for example in fruit packing, and to move inland to high pastures in the summer. On the summer pastures, the tent serves as a base camp, whilst the main herds are grazed in moving satellite camps. Camp groups may number between six to twenty five households (Bates 1973: 147). Once on the summer pastures, men tend the flocks, whilst women carry out the domestic work.

The nomadic lifestyle provides dairy and animal products: sheepskins, wool, hair, tanned hides and meat and cheese. The diet consists primarily of milk products, bread and pilaff, with meat only rarely eaten. Herds are more complex than is first apparent. They vary in size from about twenty five sheep and goats per household to flocks of over 100 per household (Bates 1973), and form three main kinds of flocks: nomadic, transhumant and stationary (Ryder 1983: 5,2,3), which are often difficult to distinguish. Where cattle are predominant a major product is butter, where sheep and goats are the primary stock, the main product is cheese (Tuncdelik 1963/4: 69). Several breeds of sheep are herded, and need skillful management to provide sufficient forage and to keep a balance between, for example, male yearlings raised for sale as meat, and a reproductive herd of stock (Ryder 1983: 222ff). The Yoruk in turn buy cultivated grains: barley, wheat straw etc. as additional foodstuffs for their stock. Farmers may also pay nomads to graze on their stubble, after harvesting, in order to provide manure for the fields (Khazanov 1984: 34-5).

Sheep stealing is a perpetual problem (the negative side of mobility), and relations between nomads and settled peoples, particularly during migration when animals may eat crops, and on the *yayla*, when relations between nomadic groups may be antagonistic, are some of the difficulties involved in this lifestyle. On the *yayla* a shepherd, armed against wolves, may tend the flocks of an entire village or small town, and sleep in a shelter in the stone sheepfold; families may also tend their herds from their tents.

Linking collections with other black tent dwellers

Tracing black tent-dwelling societies eastwards from Turkey, the collections contain several small but significant examples of material culture from various nomadic peoples as follows:[5]

From the Iraq/Iran border, a collection of about sixty items of Kurdish clothing, including complete outfits from a chief and a farmer, and daggers, was made by C. J. Edmonds in 1925. Edmonds collected in the

71

villages of Pizhoar, Mangur, Mamish and Ujaq between latitudes 36 and 36 30', and wrote his experiences up in several publications (1957), on the Kurds and Lurs of this region and in Turkey. At this time these peoples had given up nomadism and were settled farmers. This collection is supplemented by a donkey whip, and a floor felt from the Burkett Collection. Edmonds also collected six items of men's clothing from settled Lurs in Dizful.

The Bedouin of Arabia and Jordan are represented by a collection of about forty objects which consists of men's clothing, two factory-made tent mats, and three prayer mats. Additional objects in the main Arabian collection which might be included are: coffee making equipment and weapons.

Nomadic material from Afghanistan consists of four items of women's clothing from the Gilzai Kuchis; and material from the Burkett Collection: ten floor felts, four furnishings, hangings etc., four animal trappings, and two hats derived from Uzbek/Lakai and Ersari Turkmen either tent dwelling in yurts and black tents, or settled in towns along the northern border. Also sixteen items of clothing from the Baluch: Mondrani and Kalpar Bugti were acquired by the museum in the late 1950s and early 1960s.

Notes

1. Objects in the Turkish collections which are most likely to have been nomadic in provenance, include a leather water bottle 13.12.68/644, a donkey saddle 1974.291, donkey girth 1976.602, saddlebags 5.10.62/37a-b, 1982.447, a Kurdish man's cap, and a Kurdish bag and bracelet 1976.599-601. Some objects in the archaeological section of the Turkish collection are perhaps nomad- related: a bronze axehead dated late 2nd millennium BC 13.3.63/1; a floor felt sample from Beycesultan dated to the 2nd millennium BC HM 1984.56.
   Specifically provenanced nomadic objects include the Brown Collection: two large storage sacks, *cuval*, a cover, *ortu*; and a 'pillow', *yastik*, for a divan 1981.605-608; all made and used by semi-nomadic Yoruk. The Burkett collection: three women's woollen cloths, three hats and a hood, four shepherds' capes, *kepenek*, a pair of insoles, a bag, a charm, two floor felts, two camel's headdresses, a donkey or horse band, and two breech straps 1983.43, 126-8; 1984.57-8, 61, 62, 64-76. The Teague collection: a black tent, three tents, yurts, and parts of yurts, their furnishings: flat and pile woven textiles, including two tulu; felt rugs and hangings, domestic utensils, cradles, clothing and a saddle and other animal trappings 1991.10-91; 1994.97-102; 1995.40.1-67, 41-98.
   The Steel collection, 1991.97-372, consists of a range of bowls, jugs and dishes which illustrate stages of production and the main types of ceramic wares.

2. Other peoples include: Vlachs, Bedouin, Muslim 'Tatars' a nomadic Mongol people from south Russia (Lewis 1991: 190, 192); Nogay Turks from the Kuban in south Russia (Eberhard 1953: 53); 'Ulas' - despised as 'Arabs' and 'Kurds' by the Tacirli Turkomen (Eberhard 1953: 51); Cerkes from Circassia, Cecen from Bulgaria, and Uzbeks (Eberhard 1953: 52-3, 62), and there is a recently established community of refugee Kyrgyz near Lake Van.

3. There are various ways to transliterate this name: Turcoman (Persian), Turkomans, Turkmen, Turkmens etc.

4. These collections include: a scratch plough, ox-yokes, threshing board and rakes 1991.16, 41-3; 1995.95-6, 98.

5. Kurds, Iraq/Iran border: about sixty items of clothing and daggers 16.1.68/3/3-57; 1970.328-34, donkey whip 1981.376,

floor felt 1984.79. Lur, Iran: six items of men's clothing 1968.37-42. Bedouin, Arabia and Jordan: about forty objects - men's clothing 1.12.59/8-16, OS1-4, 4.1.67/2-10, two factory-made tent mats 1969.4-5, three prayer mats 1969.6-8. Additional objects in the main collection include: coffee making equipment 1.12.59/1-5; 6.12.65/129, and weapons 4295, 14.91, 15.104, 15.111, 22.12.53/11, 18.8.55. Afghanistan: four items of women's clothing, Gilzai Kuchis 21.10.60/1-3a-b, ten floor felts, four furnishings, hangings, four animal trappings, and two hats 1983.30-36, 44-46; 1984.46-55, Uzbek/Lakai and Ersari Turkmen.

Tibet

The nomadic material within the main Tibetan collection numbers about 160 or more objects, although again the boundary between nomadic and settled material culture cannot always be sharply defined. As is found elsewhere, many objects are used in common by nomads and settled people, particularly religious objects.

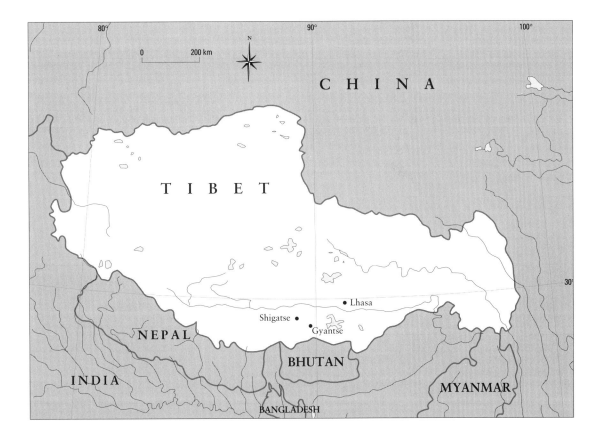

Map 7: Tibet

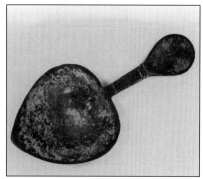

Figure 37: Spoon, Tibet
(Photograph: Horniman Museum)

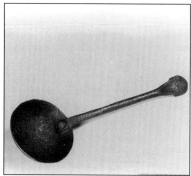

Figure 38: Ladle, Tibet
(Photograph: Horniman Museum)

Figure 39: Tea strainer, Tibet
(Photograph: Horniman Museum)

Figure 40: Teapot, brass and wood, Tibet
(Photograph: Horniman Museum)

Figure 41: Teapot, Western Tibet
(Photograph: Horniman Museum)

Figure 42: Water flask, Tibet
(Photograph: Horniman Museum)

Figure 43: Pack Saddle, Tibet
(Photograph: Horniman Museum)

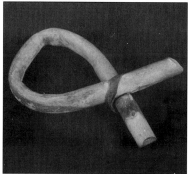

Figure 44: Yak's nose ring
(Photograph: Horniman Museum)

Figure 45: Strike-a-light, Tibet
(Photograph: Horniman Museum)

Figure 46: Far left: Woman's head ornament, Tibet (Photograph: Horniman Museum)

Figure 47: Left: Earrings, Tibet (Photograph: Horniman Museum)

The main collectors of Tibetan nomadic material have been Aris who collected among Goloks of the Ngure Lhade District in eastern Tibet (1986); and Teague who collected from refugee Drok'pa and Khambas in west central Nepal and Kathmandu (1981, 1982, 1983, 1985); other collectors include Samson, Hyatt, Tibet House, Delhi; and the Durham University Expedition.

The collection contains several tents: two black yak hair tents, a white cotton tent decorated with Buddhist symbols in appliqué, and four model tents; clothing; containers and utensils for food preparation; camping and firemaking equipment; animal trappings for horse and yak; religious material; weapons; and braid weaving equipment.[1]

The contents of the Tibetan black tent, *banag*, consist of storage bags made of woven straw and hide; a hanger; sheepskin rugs; a saddle and tack; yak hair ropes, milking pail; cream separator; bellows; a stove; cooking pots and a spatula; and food boxes.

Black tents are made from yak hair which is loosely woven in strips on a horizontal loom. The strips are then sewn together to form the tent cover. As the lower edges of the tent covers become worn, new strips are sewn on at the centre opening, so that the tent seems to 'grow'. There are several forms of black tent. The Museum's black tent is about 7 metres long x 4 metres wide x 2.5 metres high.

The internal space of the black tent is divided into two halves corresponding with the roof opening along the front-back axis. Entry is at the front beside the centre pole; the Buddhist altar place is at the right rear corner, and prized possessions are stacked along its right-hand side. The women's area is along the left hand side where they keep the kitchen utensils. Here they sit and work, for example at butter and cheese making. The central hearth is where the men and guests are entertained. Flint, steel and tinder were a common way to light a fire before matches were available. The left front corner of the tent is where fuel is stored.

Nomadic diet consists of dairy products, ground barley flour or *tsampa*, tea and meat, a family may eat up to 20 sheep per year. Animals are butchered by younger men who relinquish this duty as they grow older because of the shame Buddhists associate with such activity. Women collect the 'milk harvest' from the herds all of their lives. The material culture of food preparation largely deals with processing dairy products: milk containers or buckets; milk separators (a modern addition;) butter churns, spoons and ladles. The staple diet also includes *tsampa*, ground, roasted barley flour, which is mixed with a little tea into a dough. Tibetan tea preferably has salt, soda and butter added for taste and is prepared in a churn, then strained into a teapot and served in teabowls or into a teacup with a stand. Tea may be carried in bags as leaf or more commonly kept as bricks. Associated objects include waterbottles, food baskets, bowls, food pouches and boxes.

Tibet is about the size of Scandinavia and is mostly at an altitude of four to five thousand metres above sea level, with still higher mountains on three sides. It is one of the most difficult of all physical environments in the world to support human habitation. Where possible, subsistence is based on cultivation, barley and wheat are grown in the south, mostly in river valleys. At altitudes where crops cannot be grown livestock are crucial. Tent dwelling nomads form about half the population of Tibet, and their herds of yaks, sheep and horses, have been called, 'fields on the hoof' (Ekvall 1968).

A few Tibetan nomads wander perpetually without any territorial boundaries, but most live the year round in their black tents on particular pastures while many others are now settled on collectives social and economic organisation is based on individual household communities (Ekvall 1968: 25ff; Goldstein and Beall 1989; Khazanov 1984). The ideal is that the household head or grandparents keep the main tent at the year-round home base, while their children or hired shepherds take the livestock to satellite camps on new pastures. These camps are usually no more than two days walk away from the base camp and are specialised according to the stock herded, for example as a yak camp, a sheep-goat camp etc. Descent is reckoned through the male ('bone') line, and paternity gives one membership of a social group. Family units usually consist of a nuclear family, often extended to include a grandparent or aunt. These form a named household from which an individual may take his name, rather than having a personal name. Links between communities are usually wide ranging as a result of prohibitions on marrying relatives and a preference for exogamy. Nomads are usually monogamous, although polyandry is also practised. If a man marries into a family, the wife usually retains control of the stock. When a wife marries into another family she takes only her jewellry with her. Married women wear more jewellry than single women, and men also wear earrings and finger rings, which often function as amulets.

Figure 48: Right: Spirit scares, Tibet

Figure 49: Centre: Amulet *gau*, Tibet

Figure 50: Far left: Amulet *gau*, Tibet
(Photographs: All Horniman Museum)

The Golok of Amdo in eastern Tibet make a seasonal migration to uplands of about 4 - 5,000 metres from their lowland winter quarters. The men graze yak, sheep and goats, and hunt from base and satellite camps; they also pitch the tent, repair it and make ropes and belts. The women milk the animals, make butter and cheese, cook and work around the tent, and bring the yaks into shelter. Livestock is herded both on foot and from horseback.

It is not known when the yak was domesticated; at present wild yaks are found in Tibet, Nepal and the Himlalayas. Yaks are used for riding, as pack transport, and, when crossed with cattle, for ploughing; they provide wool, hair, milk and meat. Yak trappings include: nose rings, harness, a hobble, from Ladakh, a yak driver's bag, a string bag made of yak hair from, *Dingri*, a diorama of a yak and driver in the Himalayas; and two model yaks, a male and a female, Tibetan, from Kalimpong.

Horse trappings include: a bridle and bit, bell and band, reins, a head decoration; a saddle, saddle blanket, and girth, Eastern Tibet; a pair of saddle carpets, dated 1940, *Khamba*; a single saddle carpet, and two pairs of stirrups, one pair are *Khamba*, from eastern Tibet; a wooden pack-saddle frame and saddle bags.

Figure 51: Prayer Wheel, Tibet
Photograph: Horniman Museum)

Nomadic clothing consists of robes, *chuba*, which may be made from sheepskin, heavy woollen cloth or felt. In warm weather the right sleeve may be thrown off to expose the shoulder, and at night the *chuba* is used as a sleeping bag. Possessions such as tea bowls and eating utensils are usually carried in the pouch or fold above the waist sash. The robe is worn with a hat, shirt, and boots, usually with hide soles and cloth uppers tied with braid garters; married women wear striped cloth aprons.

Both men and women spin, often while they are walking, and men sew the tent cloth which is hard heavy work. In the traditional nomadic context only women weave cloth, but in the current refugee context many men from a formerly nomadic background are employed in the weaving industry in South Asia.

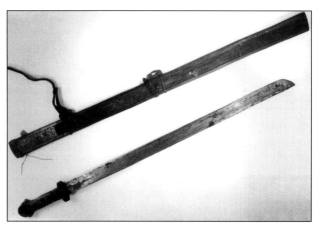

Figure 52: Sword and Sheath, Tibet
(Photograph: Horniman Museum)

Tibetans are Buddhists, with some mixture of folk beliefs, often termed *Bon*. Religious material in the collection overlaps with that from settled communities, but nomads do visit monasteries and itinerant lamas visit nomads to perform rituals such as exorcism, to read prayers, and to teach Buddhism, using a scroll painting, *thanka*, such as the Wheel of Life. On a daily basis nomads wear protective amulets, *gau*, against demonic forces. Relevant religious material, which is not a complete inventory of all such material in the collection, includes a model lama's tent; a *Gelugpa* (Yellow) hat and robe; a lama's painted leather crown, a hat with Buddhist emblems, a portable altar, a pencase; ritual vessels and a variety of apparatus such as bells, thunderbolts, *dorjes*, ritual daggers, *phurbu*, horns, *tun'vra*, books, drums, *thankas*, spirit scares, and a ghost trap; all of which indicate something of the extent of the religious items in the collection.

In the 7th and 8th centuries AD Tibet was a major power in central Asia and defeated both Chinese and Muslim armies. After the adoption of Buddhism, Tibet became pacified and was eventually ruled by the 'Yellow Hat', *Gelugpa*, monastic order led by the Dalai Lama, with the help of the nobility. Monks were drawn from all classes of society, and religion permeated the entire culture.

Trade for manufactured goods, especially silks, and commodities such as tea and tobacco has been an important part of the Tibetan economy for centuries. In the past the peoples of the borderlands: *Goloks*, *Khambas* and others often raided the great trading caravans which travelled between the Tibetan monasteries and cities, and China.

In 1950 the newly-Communist Chinese occupied Tibet. As their repression, of Buddhism increased, thousands of Tibetans, led by the Dalai Lama and nomadic Khambas and Drok'pa, became refugees in Nepal and India, where the nomads formed guerrilla bands to fight the Chinese until they were eventually disarmed and settled in camps. Repression of the Tibetans in Tibet, especially religious suppression, has been extremely severe and continues to be so. The Tibetan people are also under pressure from large-scale Chinese immigration into their country; all of which threatens and undermines their cultural and ethnic identity.

Tibetan nomads formerly regarded their black tents as defining their ethnic identity in contrast to neighbouring peoples such as Mongolians, even though the Tibetan black tent was recognised as inferior to the Mongolian *ger* in terms of warmth and comfort. The Museum's collection also includes a tent made in white cotton with applique decoration of Buddhist symbols, colours and prayer flags. This tent was made to commission by a refugee tentmaker in the Kathmandu Valley in 1984. Such tents were formerly used by wealthier people for picnics and residence during summer festivals, and as a travelling tent, and so indicated traditional beliefs and social organisation. The Chinese authorities now often require that nomads also use white tents, *khakur*, for residence and storage, instead of black tents.

Notes

1. The entire Tibetan collection consists of about 500 objects. Of these about 140 objects are more specifically nomadic. It is perhaps not possible to divide this collection sharply between those objects used by nomadic and settled peoples. The Tibetan collection contains: two black yak hair tents 1986.187, 1986.188, a white cotton tent 1985.188, and four model tents 1982.459, 1983.18-20. The contents of the East Tibetan black tent, *banag*, (1986.187) consist of storage bags made of woven straw and hide, a hanger; sheepskin rugs; a saddle and tack; yak hair ropes, milking pail; cream separator; bellows; a stove;

cooking pots and a spatula; and food boxes 1988.3-16, 21, 52.

Flint, steel and tinder 6.12.65/67; 1974.14; 1981.422, 1985.13; bellows, 1982.325. Milk containers or buckets 1988.7I-ii, 1988.61; butter churns 1983.21, NN; butter spoon 19.5.48/328; brass ladle 27.8.52/23; two copper ladles 19.5.48/374, NN546; wooden ladle 1983.21; butter box 1982.319, tea strainer 1982.326, teapot, wood, brass 27.8.52/100; teabowls 1974.13, 19.5.48/345, 371; NN 1205, 1985.14, teacup and stand 1974.13; Tea bag, *Drok'pa*, Nepal 1982.321; tea brick 1982.327. Associated material includes waterbottles 1979.15, NN; food basket 1985.132; food bowl with lid, Tibetan *Drok'pa*, Nepal 1985.197; and food pouches, *Drok'pa*, Nepal 1982.322.

Yak trappings: yaks' nose rings 19.5.48/305; 1985.190; yak harness 1985.189i-iii); a yak hobble, Ladakh 1985.21; yak driver's bag 1985.192; string bag (yak hair), *Dingri*, Tibet 1994.229); a diorama of a yak and driver in the Himalayas 1982.497; and two model yaks, a male and a female, Tibetan, *Kalimpong* 1989.103-4.

Horse trappings: bridle and bit, bell and band, reins, decoration 1982.336-339, 1985.147, 1985.194; saddle, saddle blanket, and girth, Eastern Tibet 1988.16; saddle carpets, 1940, *Khamba* 1974.242-3, saddle carpet 1990.229; stirrups 28.3.52/9; pair of stirrups, *Khamba*, Tibet 1982.342; wooden pack-saddle frame and saddle bags 1982.340-341.

Nomadic clothing includes robes, chuba, sheepskin 1988.3, woollen cloth 1982.309; felt coat and hat 6.12.65/573-4, sash 1982.314, hat 1982.313, shirt 1982.312, boots braid garters 1982.303-4, 1982.310-11; 1983.19, 1984.19, 1989.90-92, 1990.230; married women wear striped cloth aprons - apron set and brass clasp, western Tibet 1982.305-8. Married women wear more jewellry than single women, and men also wear earrings and finger rings 1982.315. Braid looms and strips 19.5.48/310, 1982.332-3; 1985.145-146; needle cases 19.5.48/376, *Drok'pa* 1982.335, 1985.198.

Associated religious material, which is not a complete inventory of all such material in the total collection, includes a model lama's tent 1983.20; a Gelugpa hat and robe 1952; a lama's painted leather crown 1979.14, a hat with Buddhist emblems 16.10.54, a portable altar 1952, ritual vessels 6.12.65/74 and various religious apparatus such as bells, *dorjes*, *phurbu*, horns, *tun'vra*, books, drums, *thankas*, spirit scares, ghost trap etc., matchlock gun NN; swords 334, HM OS 57-8, 107727.8.52/37, quiver 12.11.54/63; knife and sheath, refugee *Drok'pa*, Nepal 1982.348; *laissez passer* seal, 14th *Khamba* guerrilla army, Mustang, Nepal 1982.349.

Nomads Today

The Horniman Museum's collections of material culture from nomadic societies in Asia, like those of any museum collection, obviously cannot give a complete or total coverage of the diversity of forms and techniques employed by nomads throughout such a vast continent. Nevertheless, they provide a firm, comparative basis for future work, and an excellent resource when related to other major collections such as those held in museums in Denmark, Sweden, France, Germany and elsewhere. The Museum's collections may be assessed using three criteria: collecting, research and display.

There is a strong ethical argument for maintaining and developing the collections of Asian nomadic material culture in order to preserve a record of those peoples whose lifestyles are rapidly changing and disappearing. The Museum is currently considering proposals for a programme which includes collecting in Inner Asia and Siberia in the near future, in order to implement this aim. Significant lacunas in the Horniman collections include: black tents from the Bedouin, Qashqai, and from Afghanistan; yurts from the Kyrgyz and Kazak; a travelling tent, *maichan*, and reindeer herders' tents from Mongolia, and from Siberia. Other important material to provide a more inclusive coverage of general material culture would include objects and information relating to animal management, calculation and tallying methods, food preparation, and crafts such as leatherworking.

Exhibiting nomadic material such as tents is difficult in terms of spatial requirements, especially when a comparative approach is desirable which involves the display of several tents and their contents. The Museum has presented two such exhibitions over the last fifteen years ('Tents' in 1985-6, and 'Nomads' in 1997), with considerable success and public interest.

A different approach which the Museum has followed from time to time has been to focus on the display of a single tent with its furnishings and a greater range of contextualising material. The Mongolian collection, for example, has had considerable exposure in this manner since its acquisition in 1979. Current estimates are that about 2 million people (equivalent to the entire population of Mongolia itself) have seen this material, either at the Museum or at various festivals throughout England. These exhibitions have helped to stimulate a widespread interest in tent making and usage in Britain, which the Museum has fostered further by workshops which made a replica Kyrgyz yurt, now used for educational activities.

Research on nomadic peoples has been facilitated enormously over the last fifteen years by numerous publications, notably the magisterial works by Andrews (1997), Oliver (1997); as well as the several publications of the Carlsberg Foundation's Nomadic Research Project on individual nomadic societies in Afghanistan (Frederiksen 1996; Olesen 1994; Pedersen 1994); Luristan (Mortensen 1993), Mongolia (Boyer 1995), and Tibet (Jones 1996); and Goldstein and Beall on Tibet (n.d.) and Mongolia (1994). Scandinavian scholars have also produced journals by the Commission on Nomadic Peoples at Uppsala. Other works by German, American, British and Russian scholars are listed in the Bibliography. One hopes that the extensive literature in Russian will also soon be translated into English to make it more generally available.

Over the centuries nomads have been regarded with both fear and romance among settled peoples. Nomads have often been seen as thieves and marauders, and have fallen prey to governments which sought to control them by disarming, settling and repressing them. Nomads, and in modern society this category tends to include travellers and the homeless, continue to arouse persistent fear and unease.

A different view sees nomads as 'noble savages'. Nomads have inspired writers, artists, film-makers and ordinary people in many cultures, including those as diverse as 19th century Europe, and modern Mongolia, Japan and America, with a vision of a life of freedom and independence. Apart from the various commercial films made about Chingis (Ghengis) Khan, nomads have received extensive coverage in the 'Disappearing World' series on British television, and are well represented in the Film and Video Library of the Royal Anthropological Institute.

During the course of the twentieth century many nomads have been forced to settle and become cultivators or factory workers. This process, which occurred both in Inner and Western Asia, was particularly marked in Central Asia under Stalinist regimes which enforced settlement and collectivization with disastrous effects on peoples and herds, and was compounded by large-scale immigration of cultivators who occupied the best pasturelands, Kazakhstan provides a particular example of these social and cultural changes. Today nomadic lifestyles are threatened by many factors, including drought, political repression, economic development and modernization. Building a new railway or a canal, converting land to agricultural uses, commercial ranching and the establishment of wildlife sanctuaries may all reduce pasture lands and prevent or seriously curtail access. New patterns of tourism also bring the few remaining nomads into increasing contact with outsiders, and increase the pace of social and cultural changes which almost inevitably follow.

Recent publicity, including documentary television and film, have drawn the West's attention to the effects of social change and have increased general interest in minority groups such as nomads. Many people now count, among fundamental human rights, the right of nomadic populations to enjoy their traditional lifestyles. Organisations such as Survival International, the Minority Rights Group and UNESCO have assumed an important advocacy role in defending these lifestyles.

Museums as such cannot enter into overt lobbying of political issues in the same way assumed by advocacy groups, but they can make attempts to preserve the material culture and its associated documentation which provides informative insights into nomadic cultures, and a testament to their lifestyles. The Horniman

Museum, over the years, has presented nomadic material in exhibitions, displays and in performances by musicians and dancers from societies with former or contemporary nomadic populations. The Museum's involvement in such activities has made its interests explicit and has led to important contacts which have enabled further collections to be made, for example in Mongolia, Tibet, Turkey and Kyrgyzstan.

Collecting and representing nomadic peoples highlights an epistemological problem present in museums. Museums tend to work through conceptual constructs, sometimes having the characteristics of 'ideal types', 'myths' or charters. That is, both museum staff and their public often assume that particular objects are typical only of societies with a specific economic base – hunters and gatherers, or subsistence farmers for example. This form of thinking about objects and exhibitions often gives a falsely concrete or fixed impression of a society or culture, rather than showing the processes of social and cultural change and the relations within and between societies. Conversely, when museums do try to show such relationships, for example those involved in colonialism, their attempts may be perceived as propaganda. There is perhaps no solution to this problem, other than to place emphasis on particular societies in their historical circumstances, as I have tried to do here, rather than on generalisations which reinforce mythologizing and stereotypical patterns of thinking.

Nomads are often internally colonized and marginalized by their own governments and neighbouring settled peoples. Nomadic housing, dress, and belongings, major factors in cultural identity, have been and continue to be radically altered. Assessment of the content of collections and collecting policies must take these circumstances into account rather than following outmoded attempts to restrict collecting and display only to 'pure' or 'type' objects. Nomadic material cultures, and nomadic peoples themselves, are not so easily confined.

Appendix
Inside a Mongolian Tent

Caroline Humphrey

Mongols have socially-designated places in their tents for people and objects. Gradually, as social changes take place, the old rigid divisions are breaking up.

When a Mongol woman buys a sewing-machine, she has an allotted place in her tent to put it, and this place is the same in every tent across the steppes. This fact may seem insignificant, but it is evidence that present-day Mongols persistently categorise objects in terms of their position in space. This characteristic of Mongol life was noted by travellers as long ago as the 13th century, and it was further observed that Mongols used this categorisation to define social positions. But in the 20th century, with rapid social change, there seems to be a paradox: how can new social roles and technologically new and foreign objects be given a place in this 'traditional' system?

Mongolia was the first country after Russia to have a socialist revolution, and there have been remarkable changes since that time (1921). The slogan of party leaders was 'Let us bypass capitalism!' (Since they aimed to move directly from the pre-1921 state of feudalism to the goal of socialism). There have been many achievements: feudal Mongol society was transformed by the introduction of public ownership and the collectivisation of production: and the standard of living of the basically pastoral, nomadic population has been dramatically raised by electrical and coal industries, crop agriculture, modern medicine, and new means of communication. It is clear that of the goals seen by the fathers of the revolution, the material and administrative ones are steadily being achieved, but we know less about another aim of any socialist movement – changes in social relationship. One can get some answers by looking at new developments in the system of categorisation of objects.

Provided a system continues into the present-day, and evidence shows it does in Mongolia, then any deviation from, or addition to, the previous pattern is significant. One area of life where changes can easily be seen is in the family dwelling, the round felt tent, called *ger* – which is still used by most of the population. A young Moscow trained Mongolian ethnographer, G. Tserenxand, has recently charted these alterations over the past couple of generations in central Mongolia.

Until recently, the family was not only the main unit of ownership and production in herding, but it also organised its life in an exceptionally rigid and formal manner, closely tied to the old social conditions. Categories of age, sex, genealogical seniority, wealth, and religious status were maintained by explicit rules and prohibitions within the domestic circle. The round tent was virtually the only dwelling known in Mongolia, apart from Buddhist monasteries, and it was the focus for relationships between peoples widely separated by daily occupations. It provided a space in which every category of person or object in the nomad's world could be located, and so became a kind of microcosm of the social world of the Mongols.

In practice, the systems worked as follows. The floor area of the tent was divided into four sections, each of which was valued differently. The area from the door, which face south, to the fireplace in the centre, was the junior or low-status half, called by the Mongols the 'lower' half. The area at the back of the tent behind the fire was the honorific 'upper' part, named the *xoimor*. This division was intersected by that of the male, or ritually-pure, half, which was to the left of the door as you entered, and the female, impure, or dirty section to the right of the door, up to the *xoimor*. Within these four areas, the tent was further divided along its inner perimeter into named sections. Each of these was the designated sleeping place of people in different social roles and the correct storing place of various implements and possessions of members of the family. So closely were people identified with their objects that the wife, for example, might be known as 'cooking-pot person.'

It was considered a sin to move any utensil from its right place into another part of the tent. A woman's object was considered to pollute the men's area and a special ceremony might have to be performed to erase this. Men were not allowed to touch cooking and other 'female' things, while women were forbidden even to step over a whole range of men's goods. There was no single place in the tent where a jumbled heap of things could be put indifferently. There was even a difference in the vertical heights at which objects could be placed: some things had to be wedged behind the roof-poles, some hung from pegs in the wall –lattices, and yet others were placed on the ground.

People could move above the tent, but they had to sit, eat and sleep in their correct places. Earlier this century, among the Mongol-speaking people of Tuva, guests would be fined a horse, with harness, for insulting a host by sitting in the wrong place in his tent. This applied whether the guest over-valued or under-valued himself: it was as bad for a mediumly-ranked guest to sit in the place of an important man, as it was for him to move down a place and sit in the spot appropriate for 'clean' old people. The system was so explicit that it was possible in certain circumstances to manipulate it, as for example in the case of the lama, who, with false modesty, entered the tent on the women's side, only to provoke all the women to scream and flee from the tent and the hostess to plead, 'Honourable lama, please move further up! Please accept a seat further up.'

The effect of all this was to make the rank of each social category absolutely clear by dividing it from other categories. This process was analysed by the Soviet ethnographer S.A Tokarev. The separation of individuals within the family tent was related to the rigid division of labour in the world outside. The work of maintaining the herds and the family itself was divided more or less arbitrarily into tasks, almost all involving the use of implements (the bridle, the lasso, the milking-pail, the needle and thimble, the dung-collecting rake, the branding-iron). It is therefore not surprising that it was these items of working equipment which were used, when being stored, to symbolically differentiate between groups of people. These, and wider divisions of Mongol society, were seen in the careful seating of guests from the 'upper' to the 'lower' parts of the tent. The hierarchy was then reinforced by semi-obligatory rituals being carried out before any ordinary conversation could begin- for example, the presentation of a silk *xadag* scarf by the junior to the senior. Meals were equally formal, and women usually ate at different times from men.

Since the revolution, there have been fundamental changes. Not only have most of the old social categories gone, but new ones have appeared like factory worker, school teacher party official, veterinarian, or truck-driver. Yet comparison can still take place since people still life in family groups in the felt tent.

It seems to me, and Tserenxand's material also shows this, that the basic structure has remained, in the sense that the Mongols still have socially designated places in the tent for people and objects, and give them values. Some manufactured objects are simply merged into traditional categories. These are always objects whose function is equivalent to a traditional function. Suitcases, wardrobes and chests-of –drawers made in east Europe have replaced the old bags and painted chests: chrome-plated bedsteads take the place of felt or wooden bunks: iron buckets and china crockery are becoming more common than wooden pails and silver-lined root-wood bowls. Modern furniture is very different in materials and glossiness from Mongol's things, and it has to be squeezed into place in the low round tent, but conceptually it presents no problems.

Even if an individual herdsman's family is prosperous and has fitted out its tent in luxurious modernity, the time has not yet come when past arrangements can be forgotten. Tserenxand remarks that it is common for herdsmen on the collectives to have two tents: the 'larger *ger*' with carpets, radio, chrome beds, and so on, and the 'small *ger*' for large-scale cooking, domestic work, and storage. This small *ger* has, classically, a brazier in the centre skins on the ground, and dripping bags of sour-milk along the south west lattice wall.

But if this old pattern is at the back of people's minds, the recent changes in behaviour in relation to certain key objects seem all the more striking. The Buddhist altar, which formerly was the culmination of the entire honorific arrangement reserved for men, is now virtually never seen; it is replace either by a childrens bed or by a shelf with family photographs and ornaments. Only radically modern families take the first of these alternatives. More traditionally-minded people find reasons ('draughts from the door') to put children elsewhere. They reserve the *xoimor* for honoured images, often substituting photographs of revolutionary leaders, heroes, or family members, for pictures and statues of Lamaist deities. Children traditionally slept on the ground, beside their parents' bed. But this is now thought to be inadequate. In Mongolia today, as in other socialist countries, children are given priority in welfare and health spending; large families are encouraged; and young people are given pride of place in marches an parades, since they symbolise the future.

During the daytime, when there are guests, children are expected to stay by their mother on the east side of the tent, or go outside. The *xoimor* is again occupied by adults, usually men, with honoured guests such as officials of the collective or party sitting to the host's right. The ranking of visitors from the *xoimor* to the door is retained. Some occupations are given more respect than others' administrators, or herdsmen seem to be given a higher place than artisans, people in service industries, or working women, but this matters less than the attainment and age of the individual. Thus a wise and senior herdsman or milkmaid would be given precedence over a young party official, who had yet to prove himself. But the rituals showing clear differences in rank, such as the presenting of the *xadag*, are now thought to belong mainly to the past, or to very formal occasions. On the other hand, rituals by which Mongols visiting one another used to establish mutual friendly relations are still virtually obligatory; the exchange and mutual admiring of snuff-bottles is still so common that everyone keeps a bottle even if they do not like snuff.

These examples are about a change in social roles, but this use of material culture may be changed by a different evaluation of traditional objects. Take books, for example. In former times, books were appropriate only for lamas and senior men, since they were seen as holy receptacles for religious truth and sacred history. They were kept in the senior male part of the *xoimor*, if not on the Buddhist altar itself; and, wrapped in several layers of silk, they were read only on special occasions. Women were forbidden to read them. There was a saying 'For a woman to look at a book is like a wolf looking at a settlement.' But, since the revolution, literacy has been one of the most important government policies and no virtually all families possess some books. These are kept together in a shelf by the head of the parents' bed on the woman's side.

Then, finally, there are objects which by their very existence transform the old categories inside the tent. An example is the washstand. Washing used to be almost non-existent, perhaps because of a scarcity of water in the steppes, and it was also regarded as ritually wrong, since it might pollute the spirits or water. The idea that there might be special equipment for washing, and that all the family might wash at the same place, is a completely new one in Mongol culture, but it has recently been pressed strongly by public health authorities. Many people now have a washstand (a portable tank of water with an outlet over a basin), which is placed next to the door on the left – i.e., in the male half and opposite to the place where the wife wipes her dirty utensils. The saddle and harness which used to be kept in this place are either moved further up the wall, r put in the small *ger*. By its presence the washstand creates a space which is available to all- and this is new.

It is because the practice of categorising social relationships by manipulating objects in the space of the tent still occurs, that we can know certain social changes are taking place; the evaluation of certain occupations has changed, the attainment of individuals, including women, is valued over occupation and children are given increased symbolic importance. Mutual respect rather than hierarchy is emphasised with guests, and within the family there are many more occasion on which individuals act together —for instance, in communal meals. Some of the old divisions seem destined to disappear, like the rigid distinction between the men and women's sides of the tent, but others characteristic of the new society may take their place. Whereas, in our society the presence and distribution of objects indicates class and other differences, in Mongolia, they now show that a family, is more or less, 'progressive.'

The Traditional Tent

1) Saddle, lasso, hobbies; in winter this area might be used for young animals; at night time beggars, widows, old bachelors and ill people might be allowed to sleep here.

2) Bridle, halter and other harness hanging on peg.

3) Preparation of sour mare's milk in leather bag.

4) Preparation of yoghurt; in front of this place sat 'clean' (ie having taken a vow of sexual abstinence) old men and women.

5) The lace for storing felt, skins, blankets, bought food-stuffs; in front of this sat junior male guests towards the door and middling guests towards the *xoimor*.

6) One or two chests belonging to the male head of the household containing his clothes, footwear and other possessions; the more valuable things in the chest towards the coimor, less valuable things and sometimes children's clothes in the chest towards the door; honoured guests sat in front of these chests.

7) Gun and other hunting equipment.

8) Mongol and Tibetan books; a distinguished lama would sit in front of this position.

9) This is the centre of the *xoimor*, which extends to numbers 8 and 10 on either side; the Buddhist altar, with paintings and statues of deities, prayer wheels, offerings, candles, lamps, perhaps holy books; in the chest under the altar were kept the most valuable things, like money, silk, jade snuff-bottles, silver cups.

10) Chest with valuable things of the wife; in front of this chest sat the male head of the household when

receiving guests; his pipe, steel and flint, knife and a teapot might be kept here for him.

11) A box for hats; children of the family sat here.

12) The marital bed made of wood or felt; at the lower end of it there might be a pen for very young children; this was the place of the mistress of the house.

13) The wife's saddle and bridle were sometimes put here.

14) Wooden bowls, plates and stores of food; daughters of the house sat here.

15) Cooking pot, brazier stand, ladle cleaning rag and bunch of grass; the youngest daughter would sit here.

16) Felt mats.

17) Low wooden table for serving tea and other food.

18) Brazier.

19) Metal box for dried dung fuel.

20) Skins on ground.

21) Door.

22) This was the 'lowest' place in the tent and barely counted as being inside it; nothing was put here except perhaps women's boots or dirty underclothes; 'black people' (i.e. people who had committed a sin, killed an animal, or were in some way polluted) sat here; dogs sat here if they were allowed into the tent at all.

The Present Day Tent

1) Washstand; this is now called the' hygenic corner'.

2) Saddle and harness, otherwise kept in 'small *ger*'.

3) Preparation of sour mare's milk in leather bag.

4) Preparation of yoghurt; in some families a writing desk is put here.

5) The children's bed, with goods stored under it and on it; the bed may have a lace cover and a curtain for privacy; in front of this bed in most families sit middling-respected male guests, but in some families when there are no visitors the whole family may sit together here.

6) Child's pram and toys.

7) Wardrobe with clothes.

8) Chest for clothes and goods of the master of the household; this chest should be one of a pair with the chest at 10.

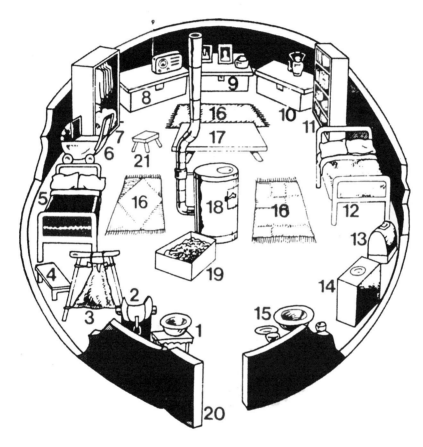

9) Chest with valuable bought things, money, silver things, electrical parts, batteries or children's bed; if there is a chest, they put framed photographs of famous people, heroes and family members here, also ornaments, prizes, diplomas.

10) Chest with womens clothes, mirror, perhaps teapot for the master of the household who usually sits in front of this place.

11) Book case.

12) The marital bed; in front of this, at the head, sits the wife with her children around her; female guests sit below, or if they are greatly respected, on the opposite side in front of the wardrobe.

13) The portable sewing machine.

14) Cupboard with china crockery.

15) Cooking pot, utensils for cooking and washing up.

16) Wool rugs.

17) Low table for serving tea and other food.

18) Iron stove, with door facing east - i.e., towards the wife's place; the chimney goes up through the smoke hole if the cooking pot is not on the stove, there is a lid.

19) Iron box for dried dung fuel.

20) Door.

21) Low stool or tiny chair for guests.

Bibliography

ANDREWS, P. A. 1997. *Nomad Tent Types in The Middle East*, Wiesbaden: Ludwig Reichert Verlag, **2vv.**

ASCHERSON, N. 1995. *The Black Sea, London*: Jonathan Cape

BACON, E. E. 1980. *Central Asians under Russian Rule,* London: Cornell University Press.

BALZER, M. M. (ed.), 1990. *Shamanism. Soviet Studies of Traditional Religion in Siberia and Central Asia,* London: M. E. Sharpe.

BARFIELD, T. J. 1989. *The Perilous Frontier. Nomadic Empires and China,* Oxford: Blackwell.

BARTH, F. 1961. *Nomads of South Persia. The Basseri Tribe of the Khamseh Confederacy,* London: Allen & Unwin.

BASILOV, V. N. (ed.), 1989. *Nomads of Eurasia,* Natural History Museum of Los Angeles County: University of Washington Press.

BATES, D. G. 1973. *Nomads and Farmers; A Study of the Yoruk of Southeastern Turkey,* Ann Arbour: University of Michigan.

BEARDSLEY, R. K. 1953. Hypotheses on Inner Asian Pastoral Nomadism and its Culture Area, *Mem. Soc. American Archaeology,* No. **9**, 24-28.

BELENITSKY, A. 1968. *Central Asia, Archaeologia Mundi,* Geneva: Nagel.

BELL, SIR CHARLES, 1928. *The People of Tibet,* Oxford: Oxford University Press.

BLACKWOOD, B. 1970. *The Classification of Artefacts in the Pitt Rivers Museum,* Oxford: Oxford University Press.

BOULNOIS, L. 1966. *The Silk Road,* London: Allen and Unwin.

BOWLES, G. T. 1977. *The People of Asia,* London: Weidenfeld & Nicolson.

BOYER, M. 1995. *Mongol Jewelry,* London: Thames & Hudson.

BURKETT, M. E. 1979. *The Art of the Feltmaker,* Kendal: Wilson.

BURNABY, F. (1898) 1985. *On Horseback through Asia Minor,* Gloucester: Alan Sutton

CAROE, O. 1967. *Soviet Empire. The Turks of Central Asia and Stalinism,* London: Macmillan.

CHODAG, T. 1988. *Tibet. The Land and the People, Beijing*: New World Press.

CLARK, G. 1961. *World Prehistory. An Outline,* Cambridge: Cambridge University Press.

CROSSLAND, R. A. 1967. *Immigrants from the North,* Cambridge Ancient History, Cambridge: Cambridge University Press.

DGPI. 1993 *Directorate General of Press & Information* . Turkey, Ankara.

DOVODOV, N. 1983. *Carpets and Carpet Products of Turkmenistan,* Ashkhabad.

DYSON-HUDSON, R. & N. 1980. *Nomadic Pastoralism, Ann. Review of Anthropology* : 9/15-61.

EBERHARD, W. 1953. *Types of Settlement in South-East Turkey,* in Sociologus N.F.1.

EDMONDS, C. J. 1957. *Kurds, Turks and Arabs,* Oxford: Oxford University Press.

EKVALL, R. B. 1968. *Fields on the Hoof; nexus of Tibetan pastoralism,* New York: Holt, Rinehart and Winston.

ELIADE, M. 1974. *Shamanism,* Princeton: Princeton University Press.

ELISSEEFF, V., 1957. Eurasia and the East, in Huyghe, R., (ed.), 1957. *Larousse Encyclopaedia of Prehistoric and Ancient Art,* London: Hamlyn.

ERTURK, K. A. (ed.), 1999. *Rethinking Central Asia,* Reading: Ithaca.

FAEGRE, T. 1979. *Tents. Architecture of the nomads,* London: John Murray.

FINLAY, M. I. 1972. *Aspects of Antiquity,* Harmondsworth: Penguin.

FORDE, C. D. 1957. *Habitat, Economy and Society,* London: Methuen.

FREDERIKSEN, B. 1996. *Caravans and Trade in Afghanistan,* London: Thames and Hudson.

FRYE, R. N. (1976) 1993. *The Golden Age of Persia,* London: Weidenfeld & Nicolson.

GAISFORD, J. (ed.), 1981. *Atlas of Man,* London: Marshall Cavendish.

GHIRSHMAN, R. 1961. *Iran,* Harmondsworth: Penguin.

GLEASON, G. 1997. *The Central Asian States. Discovering Independence,* Oxford: Westview.

GODARD, A. 1958. *The Art of Iran,* London: Allen and Unwin.

GOLDSTEIN, M. C. & BEALL, C. M. 1989. *Nomads of Western Tibet,* London: Serindia.

1994. *The Changing World of Mongolia's Nomads,* Hong Kong: The Guidebook Company Ltd.

GUNDER FRANK, A. 1992. *The Centrality of Central Asia,* Amsterdam: Vrije Universteit University Press.

HARRER, H. 1954. *Seven Years in Tibet,* New York: Dutton.

HEISER, C. B. 1990. *Seed to Civilization, The Story of Food,* London: Harvard University Press.

HERODOTUS, *The Histories,* 1961. Transl. A. de Selincourt, Harmondsworth: Penguin.

HODGES, H. 1970. *Technology in the Ancient World,* Harmondsworth: Penguin.

HUMPHREY, C. 1974. Inside a Mongolian Tent, London: *New Society* 31.10.74.
1980. Theories of North Asian Shamanism, in Gellner, E., (ed.), 1980. *Soviet and Western Anthropology,* New York: Columbia University Press, pp 243-54.

JAGCHID, S. & HYER, P. 1979. *Mongolia's Culture and Society,* Folkestone: Dawson.

JAMES, P. & THORPE, N. 1996. *Ancient Inventions,* London: M. O'Mara

JANKOVICH, M. 1971. *They Rode into Europe,* London: Harrap.

JETTMAR, K. 1964. *Art of the Steppes,* New York: Crown.

JONES, S. 1996. *Tibetan Nomads,* London: Thames and Hudson.

KANDIYOTI, D. 1977. Sex Roles and Social Change: A Comparative Appraisal of Turkey's Women, *Signs* 1977, 3, 57-73.

KALTER, J. 1984. *Arts and Crafts of Turkestan,* London: Thames and Hudson.

KHAZANOV, A. M. 1984. *Nomads and the Outside World,* Cambridge: Cambridge University Press.

KOZLOV, V. 1988. *The Peoples of the Soviet Union,* London: Hutchinson.

LANDREAU, A. N. (ed.), 1978. *Yoruk: The Nomadic Weaving Tradition of the Middle East,* Pittsburgh: Museum of Art, Carnegie Institute.

LATTIMORE, O. 1962. *Inner Asian Frontiers of China,* Boston: Beacon Books.

LEWIS, G. (tr) 1974. *The Book of Dede Korkut,* Harmondsworth: Penguin.

LEWIS, R. 1971. *Everyday Life in Ottoman Turkey,* London: Batsford.

LIU, X. 1996. *Silk and Religion,* Delhi: Oxford University Press.

LUBECK, G. et al. 1993. Use of Silk in ancient Egypt, *Nature,* v. **362,** no. 6415, 4 March 1993: 25

MONGAIT, A. L. 1961. *Archaeology in the USSR,* Harmondsworth: Penguin.

MOOREY, P. R. S. 1974. *Ancient Bronzes from Luristan,* London: British Museum Publications.

MORTENSEN, I.D. 1993. Nomads of Luristan, London: Thames and Hudson. *Nature* 4.3.93

NAZAROFF, P. S. 1952. *Hunted Through Central Asia,* London: Blackwood.

OLIVER, P. (ed.), 1997. *Encyclopaedia of Vernacular Architecture of the World,* Cambridge: Cambridge: Cambridge University Press, 3vv.

PAHLEN, COUNT K. K. 1964. *Mission to Turkestan,* Oxford: Oxford University Press.

PEDERSEN, G. 1994. *Afghan Nomads in Transition,* London: Thames and Hudson.

PEKIN, E. nd. *Turkish Flat Weaves and Carpets, Istanbul:* Minyatur Yayinlari.

PHILLIPS, E.D. 1965. *The Royal Hordes,* London: Thames and Hudson.

PIGGOTT, S. 1956. *Ancient Europe,* Edinburgh: Edinburgh University Press.

RICE, T. T. 1957. *The Scythians,* New York: Praeger.

---------- 1965. *Ancient Arts of Central Asia,* London: Thames & Hudson.

ROLLE, R. 1989. *The World of the Scythians,* London: Batsford

ROSSABI, M. 1975. *China and Inner Asia. From 1368 to the Present Day,* London: Thames & Hudson.

RYDER, M. L. 1983. *Sheep and Man,* London: Duckworth.

SIMKIN, C. G. F. 1968. *The Traditional Trade of Asia,* Oxford and London: Oxford University Press..

SINOR, D. (ed.), 1990. *The Cambridge History of Early Inner Asia,* CUP.

STEIN, R. A. 1972. *Tibetan Civilisation,* London: Faber & Faber.

SMITH, G. (ed.), 1990. *The Nationalities Question in the Soviet Union,* London: Longman.

TAPPER, R. 1979. *Pasture and politics: economics, conflict and ritual among the Shah Sevan nomads of northwestern Iran,* London: Academic Press.

TEAGUE, K. 1988. 'Portable Housing in Central Asia', in *Echoes, The Feltmakers News,* 1988/9.

---------- 1990. *Metalcrafts of Central Asia,* Aylesbury: Shire.

THOMAS, H. 1979. *An Unfinished History of the World,* London: Hamish Hamilton

THOMPSON, J. 1986. *Dobag. A return to tradition, in Hali, 30, April 1986.*

TIMES BOOKS 1996. *Past Worlds. Times Atlas of Archaeology,* London: Times Books.

TUNCDILEK, N. 1963/4. Yayla settlements and related activities in Turkey, in *Review of the Geographical Institute of the University of Istanbul,* nos. **9-10,** 58

TURNER, E. M. (ed.), 1980. *Kapchigai Defile. The Journal of Paul Nazaroff,* London: Athenaeum.

VAINSHTEIN, S. 1980. *Nomads of South Siberia,* London: Cambridge: Cambridge University Press.

VICKERS, M. 1979. *Scythian Treasures in Oxford,* Oxford: Ashmolean Museum.

WATSON, W. 1971. *Cultural Frontiers in Ancient East Asia,* Edinburgh: Edinburgh University Press.

WOLF, E. R. 1982. *Europe and the People without History,* Berkeley, Los Angeles and London: University of California Press.